CAMBRIDGE LIBRARY COLLECTION

Books of enduring scholarly value

Printing and Publishing History

The interface between authors and their readers is a fascinating subject in its own right, revealing a great deal about social attitudes, technological progress, aesthetic values, fashionable interests, political positions, economic constraints, and individual personalities. This part of the Cambridge Library Collection reissues classic studies in the area of printing and publishing history that shed light on developments in typography and book design, printing and binding, the rise and fall of publishing houses and periodicals, and the roles of authors and illustrators. It documents the ebb and flow of the book trade supplying a wide range of customers with products from almanacs to novels, bibles to erotica, and poetry to statistics.

What is an Index?

Henry Benjamin Wheatley (1838–1917) was a bibliographer and editor with a prodigious output of books and articles to his name. Brought up after the death of both his parents by his brother Benjamin Robert, himself a skilled bibliographer and cataloguer, Henry compiled catalogues for learned societies and worked for many years for the Royal Society and the Royal Society of Arts; he was a founder member of the Library Association and of the Early English Text Society, and produced an edition of Pepys' diary which was not superseded until the 1970s. This work, published in 1879, is one of two which he produced on the subject of indexing, and which led him to become known as 'the father of British indexing': the Wheatley Medal awarded by the Society of Indexers is named after him. This book shows the development of indexes (beginning with the origin of the word itself), gives rules for their compilation and provides a bibliographical list of important indexes and concordances. It remains a fascinating introduction to indexing for the professional and amateur alike.

T0382557

Cambridge University Press has long been a pioneer in the reissuing of out-of-print titles from its own backlist, producing digital reprints of books that are still sought after by scholars and students but could not be reprinted economically using traditional technology. The Cambridge Library Collection extends this activity to a wider range of books which are still of importance to researchers and professionals, either for the source material they contain, or as landmarks in the history of their academic discipline.

Drawing from the world-renowned collections in the Cambridge University Library, and guided by the advice of experts in each subject area, Cambridge University Press is using state-of-the-art scanning machines in its own Printing House to capture the content of each book selected for inclusion. The files are processed to give a consistently clear, crisp image, and the books finished to the high quality standard for which the Press is recognised around the world. The latest print-on-demand technology ensures that the books will remain available indefinitely, and that orders for single or multiple copies can quickly be supplied.

The Cambridge Library Collection will bring back to life books of enduring scholarly value (including out-of-copyright works originally issued by other publishers) across a wide range of disciplines in the humanities and social sciences and in science and technology.

What is
an Index?

A Few Notes on Indexes and Indexers

HENRY BENJAMIN WHEATLEY

CAMBRIDGE
UNIVERSITY PRESS

CAMBRIDGE UNIVERSITY PRESS

Cambridge, New York, Melbourne, Madrid, Cape Town, Singapore,
São Paolo, Delhi, Dubai, Tokyo, Mexico City

Published in the United States of America by Cambridge University Press, New York

www.cambridge.org
Information on this title: www.cambridge.org/9781108021531

© in this compilation Cambridge University Press 2010

This edition first published 1879
This digitally printed version 2010

ISBN 978-1-108-02153-1 Paperback

This book reproduces the text of the original edition. The content and language reflect
the beliefs, practices and terminology of their time, and have not been updated.

Cambridge University Press wishes to make clear that the book, unless originally published
by Cambridge, is not being republished by, in association or collaboration with, or
with the endorsement or approval of, the original publisher or its successors in title.

WHAT IS AN INDEX?

A FEW NOTES

ON

INDEXES AND INDEXERS.

BY

HENRY B. WHEATLEY, F.S.A.

HON. SEC. OF THE INDEX SOCIETY, AND
TREASURER OF THE EARLY ENGLISH TEXT SOCIETY.

"I for my part venerate the inventor of Indexes; and I know not
to whom to yield the preference, either to Hippocrates, who was
the first great anatomiser of the human body, or to that unknown
labourer in literature who first laid open the nerves and arteries
of a book."—*Isaac Disraeli, Literary Miscellanies.*

"I magnify mine office."

LONDON:

PUBLISHED FOR THE INDEX SOCIETY
BY LONGMANS, GREEN & Co., 39, PATERNOSTER ROW.
MDCCCLXXIX.

SECOND EDITION.

HERTFORD :
PRINTED BY STEPHEN AUSTIN AND SONS.

TABLE OF CONTENTS.

HISTORICAL ACCOUNT.

PRACTICE OF INDEX-MAKING.

I.—COMPILATION.

II.—ARRANGEMENT.

III.—PRINTING.

WHAT IS AN INDEX?

BEFORE proceeding to answer the question that forms the title of this pamphlet, it will be necessary to say somewhat on the history of the word *Index*. It is now used very generally in English to express a table of references arranged in alphabetical order and placed either at the end or sometimes at the beginning of a book, but this is really one only of its many meanings, and moreover not the earliest one. An index is an indicator or pointer out of the position of required information, such as the finger post on a high road, or the index finger of the human hand. In this general sense the word is used by Drayton :—

> "Lest when my lisping, guilty tongue should halt,
> My lips might prove the *index* to my fault." [1]

Such is still its meaning, and it is in this sense that the Index Society would wish their title to be understood.

There is a group of words, viz. *Index, Table, Register, Calendar, Summary,* and *Syllabus,* all of which were once generally used with much the same signification ; but as soon as *Index* had been recognized as a thoroughly English word, it beat its companions in the race, although it had a long struggle with the word *Table.*

The need of some general indication of the contents of books was early felt, and Seneca, in sending certain volumes to his friend Lucilius, accompanied them with notes of particular passages, so that he, "who only aimed at the useful might be spared the trouble of examining them entire." Thus it is that many of our old MSS. contain these helpful tables of contents, which are usually headed by the Latin words *Tabula, Calendarium,* etc. In Dan Michel's *Ayenbite of Inwyt* (1340) there is a very full Table with the heading—"Thise byeth the capiteles of the boc volȝinde."

[1] *Rosamond's Epistle,* lines 103–4.

With the invention of printing many time-saving expedients were introduced, and one of these apparently was the alphabetical or arranged index.

In tracing the history of the use of the word *Index* two distinct questions have to be considered—(1) the original use of the Latin word by the Romans; and (2) the introduction of the word into the modern languages and its naturalization in English. With regard to the first question, we find that according to classical usage *Index* denoted a discoverer, discloser or informer; a catalogue or list (Seneca refers to an Index of Philosophers); an inscription; the title of a book; and the fore or index-finger, in reference to which Cicero makes a mild joke. Writing to Atticus he says that Pollex told him that he would be back by the 13th of August, and he came to Lanuvium on the 12th, thus he is rightly called *Pollex* and not *Index*, because the thumb comes before the forefinger. Cicero also uses the word to express the table of contents to a book, for he asks Atticus to send him two library clerks to repair his books, and they are to bring with them some parchment to make indexes on. Had he only used the word *Index* we might have been in doubt as to what he really meant, but fortunately he added "which you Greeks call a *Syllabus*," and the meaning thus becomes clear.[1]

As to the second question, we may infer, from the use of *Index* in the nominative instead of the accusative case, that the word came into English through literature and not through speech. The Italian word is *Indice*, which comes directly from the Latin accusative, and it is perhaps this form (though it may be the French word *Indice*) that Ben Jonson uses when he writes "too much talking is ever the *indice* of a fool."[2]

The most celebrated of Indexes, the *Index librorum prohibitorum* and *Index Expurgatorius* of the Roman Catholic Church, are not indexes in the modern acceptation of the term, but partake more of the character of what we should now call Registers. Erasmus gives alphabetical indexes to many of his

---

[1] "Etiam vellem mihi mittas de tuis librariolis duos aliquos, quibus Tyrannio utatur glutinatoribus, ad cetera administres : iisque imperes ut sumant membranulam, ex qua *indices* fiant, quos vos Græci (ut.opinor) συλλάβους appellatis."—Ad. Atticum lib. iv. ep. 4.

[2] *Discoveries*, ed. 1640, p. 93.

books, but arrangement in alphabetical order was by no means considered indispensable in an Index; thus in a curious and learned work published at Amsterdam, in 1692, we find an "Index Generalissimus" (Table of Contents); an "Index Generalis" (Synopsis of Subjects or Heads of Chapters) at the beginning of the volume, and an "Index Alphabeticus" at the end.

It is with the general meaning of a table of contents or preface that Shakespeare uses the word Index, thus Nestor says—

> " Our imputation shall be oddly poised
> In this wild action ; for the success,
> Although particular, shall give a scantling
> Of good or bad unto the general ;
> And in such *indexes*,[1] although small pricks
> To their *subsequent volumes,* there is seen
> The baby figure of the giant mass
> Of things to come at large."—*Troilus and Cressida*, i. 3.

Buckingham threatens—

> " I'll sort occasion
> As *index* to the story we late talk'd of,
> To part the queen's proud kindred from the king."—*Richard III.* ii. 2.

and Iago refers to "an *index* and obscure prologue to the history of lust and foul thoughts."—*Othello*, ii. 1.

All these passages seem clearly to illustrate the old meaning of the word, but in the following places something more appears to be meant. Queen Margaret alludes to "the flattering index of a direful pageant" (*Rich. III.* iv. 4), probably with some reference to a special setting out of the contents, like the posters for the newspapers of to-day, which usually promise far more than the papers themselves fulfil. The Queen in *Hamlet* (iii. 4) cries out—

> " Ay me, what act
> That roars so loud and thunders in the index ? "

Meaning to say—if this prologue or setting forth of what is to follow is so fierce, what will the accusation itself be ?

---

[1] I would here, under cover of our great poet's name, protest against the use of the plural *indices.* As long as a word continues to take the plural form of the language from which it is borrowed, we cannot look upon it as thoroughly naturalized. Surely Index may be considered an English word when it was treated as such by Shakespeare.

Although we find from these quotations that the word 'index' was commonly used, it was not generally introduced into books as a thorough English word until a much later period; for instance, North's translation of Plutarch's Lives, the book so diligently used by Shakespeare in the production of his Roman Histories, contains an alphabetical index at the end, but it is called a *Table*. On the title-page of Baret's *Alvearie* (1573) mention is made of "two *Tables* in the ende of this booke," but the Tables themselves, which were compiled by Abraham Fleming,[1] being lists of the Latin and French words, are headed "Index." Between these two tables, in the edition of 1580, is "an Abecedarie, *Index* or Table" of Proverbs. The word Index is not included in the body of the Dictionary, where, however, "Table" and "Regester" are inserted. Table is defined as "a booke or regester for memorie of things," and "Regester" as "a reckeninge booke wherein thinges dayly done be written." By this it is clear that Baret did not consider Index to be an English word.[2] At the end of Johnson's edition of Gerarde's Herbal (1636) is an "Index latinus" followed by a "Table of English names," although a few years previously Minsheu had given *Index* a sort of half-hearted welcome into his Dictionary. Under that word in the *Guide into Tongues* (1617) is the entry "vide Table in Booke, in litera T.," where we read "a Table in a booke or Index." Even when acknowledged as an English word, it was frequently applied to a more severe list than the analytical table; for instance, Dugdale's Warwickshire contains an "Index of Towns and Places" and a "Table of Men's Names and Matters of most note"; and Scobell's Acts and Ordinances of Parliament, 1640–1656 (publ. 1658) has "An Alphabetical Table of the most material contents of the whole book," preceded by "An Index of the general titles comprized in the ensuing Table." There are a few exceptions to the rule here set forth; for instance, Plinie's *Naturall Historie of the World*, translated by Philemon Holland (1601), has at the beginning

---

[1] My friend Mr. Furnivall draws my attention to the fact that Fleming was the index-maker of Shakespeare's day as Philemon Holland was the translator.

[2] Some in the present day seem to be of the same opinion as Baret, for we occasionally hear of an *Index Rerum* instead of an *Index of Subjects*.

—"The Inventorie or Index containing the contents of 37 bookes," and at the end "An Index pointing to the principal matters." In Speed's *History of Great Britaine* (1611) there is an "Index or Alphabetical Table containing the principal matters in this history."

About the latter half of the seventeenth century the race for supremacy between *Index* and *Table* was well-nigh closed in favour of the former, but the word Table was occasionally used up to a much later period. A very late instance occurs in the *Monthly Review* commenced in 1749. At the beginning of each volume is an alphabetical index of books reviewed called a *Table*, and at the end is an Index of the remarkable passages in the articles which is styled *Index*. By the present English usage, according to which the word *table* is reserved for the summary of the contents as they occur in the book, and the word *index* for the arranged analysis of the contents, we obtain an advantage not enjoyed in other languages, for the French *Table* is used for both kinds, as is *Indice* in Italian and Spanish.

The French word *indice* has a different meaning from the Italian *indice*, and in fact is not the same word. According to Littre it is derived from the Latin *indicium*. The word *index* in French is pretty well confined to tables of Latin and Greek, as it once was in English, although it is used by Bossuet in a more general sense. In German *Index* is occasionally used, but the regular word is *Register*.

In concluding this philological inquiry it will only be necessary to repeat the remark with which we commenced, that although the word *index* is used to express a particular kind of arranged list, it has also the wider meaning of a general indicator. Thus the words Inventory, Register, Calendar, Catalogue, Summary, and Syllabus will all find their respective places under the general heading of Index work.[1]

---

[1] Another word occasionally used in the sense of an Index is *Pye*, which has been supposed to be derived from the Greek Πίναξ. The late Sir T. Duffus Hardy, in some observations on the derivation of the word "Pye-Book," remarks that the earliest use he had noted of *pye* in this sense is dated 1547—"A Pye of all the names of such Balives as been to accompte pro anno regni regis Edwardi Sexti primo."—Appendix to the 35th Report of the Deputy Keeper of the Public Records, p. 195.

As books increased, the need of indexes could not fail to be very generally felt; but authors, while praising them, often thought it necessary to warn their readers against the dangers of mere "index learning." Thus John Glanville writes in his *Vanity of Dogmatizing:*—"Methinks 'tis a pitiful piece of knowledge that can be learnt from an index, and a poor ambition to be rich in the inventory of another's treasure." Dr. Watts alludes to those whose "learning reaches no farther than the tables of contents," but he also says, "If a book has no index or good table of contents, 'tis very useful to make one as you are reading it."

Fuller very wisely argues that the diligent man should not be deprived of a tool because the idler may misuse it. He says, "An Index is a necessary implement and no impediment of a book except in the same sense wherein the carriages [i.e. things carried] of an army are termed *impedimenta*. Without this a large author is but a labyrinth without a clue to direct the reader therein. I confess there is a lazy kind of learning which is only indical, when scholars (like adders, which only bite the horse's heels) nibble but at the tables, which are calces librorum, neglecting the body of the book. But though the idle deserve no crutches (let not a staff be used by them but on them), pity it is the weary should be denied the benefit thereof, and industrious scholars prohibited the accommodation of an index, most used by those who most pretend to contemn it." I have heard the same objection urged to-day, but surely it is a mere delusion. There are many easier means by which the sciolist may obtain a smattering of knowledge without consulting an Index. No useful information can thus be gained unless the books to which the Index refers are searched, and he who honestly searches ceases to be a smatterer.

Fuller was a true Index-connoisseur, and in his "Pisgah-sight of Palestine" (1650) he gives necessary directions for the use of the Index, where he says, "An Index is the bag and baggage of a book, of more use then honour; even such who seemingly slight it, secretly using it, if not for need, for speed of what they desire to finde." Whatever Fuller touched he made sparkle, and no one but he could have written such lively sentences as the following on a subject

usually thought to be so dry :—"And thus by God's assistance we have finished our table.   Miraculous almost was the
execution done by David on the Amalekites who saved neither
man nor woman alive to bring tidings to Gath.   I cannot
promise such exactness in our Index, that no name hath
escaped our enquiry : some few, perchance, hardly slipping
by, may tell tales against us.   This I profess, I have
not, in the language of some modern quartermasters, wil-
fully burnt any towns, and purposely omitted them ; and
hope that such as have escaped our discovering, will upon
examination appear either not generally agreed on, by authors,
for proper names, or else by proportion falling without the
bounds of Palestine.   Soli Deo gloria."   Of the same mind
with Fuller that the Index is a most important part of a
work was the Italian physician mentioned by Mdlle. de
Scudery, who dedicated each book of his Commentary on
the Aphorisms of Hippocrates to one of his friends, and
the Index to another.   Those who hold the contrary opinion
are either jealous that others will obtain their knowledge
too easily, or they do not relish the trouble of preparing
an Index.   The publisher of Howell's "Discourse concerning
the Precedency of Kings" (1664) was one of the latter class,
although he puts forward a more plausible reason for his
neglect in this letter from "The Bookseller to the Reader."
"The reason why there is no Table or Index added hereunto
is, that every page in this work is so full of signal remarks
that were they couch'd in an Index it wold make a volume
as big as the book, and so make the Postern Gate to bear no
proportion to the Building.   S. Speed."

Each generation must do its own work, and although benefit
is gained from all that has gone before, it often forgets the
obligation it is under to preceding ages.   An Index therefore is a standing warning against forgetfulness, and accurate
reference to forgotten work is almost equal to a new dis-
covery.   The value of indexes was recognized in the earliest
times, and many old books have full and admirably-con-
structed indexes; for instance, Juan de Pineda's "Monarchia
Ecclesiastica o historia Universal del Mundo," (*Salamanca*,
1588,) has a very curious and valuable table which forms the

fifth volume of the whole set ; and the three folio volumes
of Indexes in one alphabet to the *Annales Ecclesiastici* of
Baronius form a noble work.

Indexes need not necessarily be dry, and in some cases they
form the most interesting portion of a book.   The Index to
Prynne's *Histrio-mastix* (1633), unlike the text, is very read-
able, and from it may be obtained a sufficient idea of the
author's argument.   Prynne deserves especial mention here, as
he may be considered as a martyr to his conscientiousness
in producing this useful key to the contents of his ponderous
volume.   No one could read through the book, with its notes
overflowing into the margin, so the licenser got confused and
passed it in despair.   Carlyle refers to the *Histrio-mastix* as
"a book still extant but never more to be read by mortal."
The vituperation however was easily understood when boiled
down in an alphabetical form, and Attorney-General Noy found
that the author himself had forged the weapons that the pro-
secutor could use in the attack.   This is proved by a passage
in Noy's speech at Prynne's trial, where he points out that
the accused "says Christ was a Puritan in his Index." [1]
It has been observed that the author scarcely ventures on
the most trivial opinion without calling to his aid " squadrons
of authorities " from the writers of all nations, and in a book
which contains this passage—" the profession of a Play-poet
or the composing of comedies, tragedies or such like Playes
for publike players or play-houses is altogether infamous and
unlawfull," he is more ready to mention the Greek and Latin
dramatists than those of our own country. A few of the entries
in the Index are worth particular notice.   In this one the
indexer does not commit himself, but he infers much—
" Æschylus one of the first inventors of tragedies.   His strange
and sudden death."   Here are some heavy charges against
theatres—

"Idleness, a dangerous mischevous sin occasioned and fomented by
stage plays.
Impudency, a dangerous sin occasioned by stage plays.
Lyes condemned, frequent in plays.
Sedition occasioned by stage plays."

[1] Noy calls it an Index, but Prynne, in conformity with the usual practice, writes
Table.

The index is full of the judgments which are supposed to follow the acting of plays, of which the following are specimens :—

"Herod Agrippa smitten in the theater by an angel and so died.

Herod the great, the first erecter of a theater among the Jews, who thereupon conspire his death.

Plagues occasioned by stage plays. All the Roman actors consumed by a plague.

Theatres overturned by tempests."

The author appears to have been very conversant with the doings of the unseen worlds, for he writes—

"Crossing of the face when men go to plays shuts in the Devil.

Devils, inventors and fomentors of stage plays and dancing. Have stage plays in hell every Lord's day night.

Heaven—no stage plays there."

In the following entry the word *and* probably seemed most natural to Prynne :—

"Players, many of them Papists *and* most desperate wicked wretches."

But it was the strong terms in which women actors are denounced, and such entries as the following, that gave the greatest offence to the Court :[1]—

"Acting of popular or private enterludes for gain or pleasure infamous, unlawfull, and that as well for Princes, Nobles, Gentlemen, Schollars, Divines as common actors.

Kings—infamous for them to act or frequent Playes or favour Players."

The Indexer has a considerable power in his hand if he chooses to use it, for he can state in a few words what the author may have hidden in verbiage, and he can so arrange his materials as to force the reader to draw an inference. Macaulay knew how an author's own words might be turned against himself, and therefore he wrote to his publishers, "Let no d—— Tory make the Index to my History." In the Index to the eighth volume of the

---

[1] The book was published six weeks before Henrietta Maria acted in a pastoral at Somerset House, so that the passage "women actors notorious whores" could not have been intended to allude to the Queen. See Cobbett's "State Trials," vol. 3, coll. 561–586.

Quarterly Journal of Science, Literature, and the Arts, 1820, is
the following entry :—

"Watts (Mr.), illiberal remarks of, on Captain Kater's experiments."

Mr. Watts was displeased at the use of the uncomplimentary
adjective and complained to the Editor.   In the Notices to
Correspondents at the beginning of the tenth volume we read:
—"The Editor begs to apologize to Mr. Watts for the term
'illiberal' used in the index of vol. 8 of this Journal.   It
escaped his observation till Mr. Watts pointed it out."   Mr.
Hill Burton, in his *Book Hunter,* very justly observes of a
controversialist that after almost exhausting his weapons of
attack in the preface, and in the body of the book, "if he be
very skilful he may let fly a few Parthian arrows from the
Index."   The witty Dr. William King, Judge of the Irish
Court of Admiralty, was one of the first to see how formidable
a weapon of attack the Index might be made, and Disraeli
calls him the inventor of satirical and humorous indexes.
His earliest essay in this field was the index added to the
second edition of that clever but shallow work written by
the Christ Church wits in the name of the Hon. Charles
Boyle — "Dr. Bentley's Dissertation on the Epistles of
Phalaris and the Fables of Esop examin'd," 1698.   The
first entry is

"Dr. Bentley's true story of the MS. prov'd false by the testimonies of
              Mr. Bennet p. 6
              Mr. Gibson p. 7
              Dr. King p. 8
              Dr. Bentley p. 19;"

then comes "his modesty and decency in contradicting great
men," followed by the names of Plato, Selden, Grotius,
Erasmus, Scaliger, and ending with *everybody.*   The last
entry is—"his profound skill in criticism; *from beginning to
end.*"   After the publication of this book there was silence
for a time which caused some to suppose that Bentley was
beaten, but at last appeared the 'immortal' *Dissertation,* as
Porson calls it, which not only defeated his enemies, but positively annihilated them.   In the same year that King assisted
Boyle he turned his attention to a less formidable antagonist

than the great Bentley. His *Journey to London*, 1698, is a very ingenious parody of Dr. Martin Lister's *Journey to Paris*, and the pages of the original being referred to, it forms an Index to that book. Sir Hans Sloane was another of Dr. King's butts, and the *Transactioneer* (1700) and *Useful Transactions in Philosophy* (1708–9) were very galling to the distinguished naturalist, and annoyed the Royal Society, whose *Philosophical Transactions* were unmercifully laughed at. To both these tracts were prefixed satirical contents, and what made them the more annoying was that the author's own words were very ingeniously used and turned against him. King writes, "The bulls and blunders which Sloane and his friends so naturally pour forth cannot be misrepresented, so careful I am in producing them." Such an effective mode of annoyance, when once discovered, was not likely to be overlooked, and we find it used soon afterwards with a political object. William Bromley, a Tory Member of Parliament and high churchman, had made the grand tour in early life, and published "Remarks made in his Travels in 1693." In 1705 he was a candidate for the Speakership, and his opponents took the opportunity of reprinting his Travels with a satirical Index as an electioneering squib. This Index is very amusing, and in some instances the text bears it out, but in others there is a malicious perversion. The following are a selection from the entries :—

"Chatham, where and how situated, viz. on the other side of Rochester bridge, though commonly reported to be on this side, p. 1.

Boulogne, the first city on the French shore, lies on the coast, p. 2.

Crosses and crucifixes on the roads in France prove it not England, p. 3.

Eight pictures take up less room than sixteen of the same size, p. 14.

February an ill season to see a garden in, p. 53.

Three several sorts of wine drank by the author out of one vessel, p. 101.

The English Jesuites Colledge at Rome may be made larger than 'tis by uniting other Buildings to it, p. 132.

The Duchess dowager of Savoy who was grandmother to the present Duke was mother to his father, p. 243.

An university in which degrees are taken, p. 249.

In the Bodleian copy of this book there is a MS. note by Dr. Rawlinson to the effect that this index was drawn up by

Robert Harley Earl of Oxford, but this was probably only a party rumour. Dr. Parr possessed Bromley's own copy of the reprint with a MS. note—"This edition of these travels is a specimen of the good nature and good manners of the Whigs, and I have reason to believe of one of the Ministry very conversant in this sort of calumny. . . . . This printing my book was a very malicious proceeding; my words and meaning being very plainly perverted in several places. . . . . But the performances of others . . . . may be in like manner exposed as appears by the like tables published for the travels of Bishop Burnet and Mr. Addison." Bromley was elected Speaker in 1710.

That the love for a humorous index has not quite died out is proved by the admirable one which Mr. Lowell has added to his *Biglow Papers.* Where all is good it is not easy to select, and I feel forced to make a long extract :—

> "Adam, eldest son of, respected.
> Babel, probably the first congress.
> Birch, virtue of, in instilling certain of the dead languages.
> Cæsar, a tribute to, 99, his *veni, vidi, vici* censured for undue prolixity, 116.
> Castles, Spanish, comfortable accommodations in.
> Eating words, habit of, convenient in time of famine.
> Longinus recommends swearing (Fuseli did same thing).
> No, a monosyllable, 51, hard to utter, *ib.*
> Noah inclosed letter in bottle, probably.
> Ulysses, husband of Penelope, 58, borrows money, 135. (For full particulars see Homer and Dante).
> Wrong, abstract, safe to oppose." [1]

The occupation of the indexer has been allowed to fall into disrepute during the present century, and some have supposed that any ignorant hack can produce this indispensable portion of a book. Such was not always the case, for most old books of any mark have indexes of a high character, which clearly show that both author and publisher took a proper

---

[1] This is the last entry but one in the index, and I cannot resist the pleasure of adding in a note the passage here indexed :—
> " I'm willin a man should go tollable strong
>   Agin wrong in the abstract, for that kind o' wrong
>   Is ollers unpop'lar an' never gits pit'ed,
>   Because it's a crime no one never committed."

pride in this part of their work. This spirit found whim-
sical expression in the speech of a once celebrated Spaniard
quoted by the great bibliographer Antonio—that the index
of a book should be made by the author, even if the book
itself were written by some one else.[1] An ideal indexer needs
many high qualifications; but, unlike the poet, he is not born
but made. He must be a good analyser and know how to
reduce the author's many words into a terse form. He must
also be continually thinking of the wants of the consulter of
his index, so as to place his references under the heading
that the reader is most likely to seek. If he does his work
well he will have many appreciative readers ; for, as Henry
Rogers has observed, "no writer is so much read as the
maker of a good index—or so much cited." Dr. Allibone
prints in his valuable Dictionary of Authors (vol. i. p. 85), an
extract from a number of the Monthly Review, which is well
worthy of quotation here :—"The compilation of an index
is one of those useful labours for which the public, commonly
better pleased with entertainment than with real service, are
rarely so forward to express their gratitude as we think they
ought to be. It has been considered as a task fit only for
the plodding and the dull : but with more truth it may be said
that this is the judgment of the idle and the shallow. The
value of anything, it has been observed, is best known by
the want of it. Agreeably to this idea, we, who have often
experienced great inconveniences from the want of indices,
entertain the highest sense of their worth and importance.
We know that in the construction of a good index, there is
far more scope for the exercise of judgment and abilities, than
is commonly supposed. We feel the merits of the compiler
of such an index, and we are ever ready to testify our thank-
fulness for his exertions."

The eminent bibliographer William Oldys expressed a very
similar sentiment in words which have been printed by Mr.
Thoms in *Notes and Queries* (2nd series, vol. xi. p. 309):

---

[1] " Idcirco celebris quidam scriptor nostræ gentis, quò significaret eam curam ejus
esse debere, cujus cura opus ipsum constitit, urbane, salseque ajebat, Indicem libri
ab authore, librum ipsum a quovis alio conficiendum esse."—Nicolaus Antonius,
Bibliotheca Hispana, 1672, tom. 2, p. 371.

"The labour and patience, the judgment and the penetration which are required to make a good index, is only known to those who have gone through this most painful, but least praised part of a publication. But as laborious as it is, I think it indispensably necessary to manifest the treasures of any multifarious collection, facilitate the knowledge to those who seek it and invite them to make application thereof."

We can point to a goodly roll of eminent men who have not feared this labour and who have not been ashamed to appear before the world as indexers. In the first rank we must place the younger Scaliger, who devoted ten months to the compilation of an elaborate index to Gruter's magnificent *Thesaurus Inscriptionum.* Bibliographers have been unanimous in praise of the energy exhibited by the great critic in undertaking so vast a labour. Antonio describes the index as an herculean work, and Le Clerc observes that if we think it surprising that so great a man should undertake so laborious a task, we must remember that such indexes can only be made by a very able man. Nicolas Antonio, the compiler of one of the fullest and most accurate bibliographies ever planned, whose name has already been mentioned in these pages, was a connoisseur in indexes and wrote a short essay on the makers of them. His *Bibliotheca Hispana* is not known so well as it deserves to be on account of the little general interest that is taken in Spanish literature, but having some years ago used it almost daily, I can speak of it with gratitude as one of the most trustworthy of works. The system upon which the authors' names are arranged is one that at first sight might seem to give cause for ridicule; for they appear in an alphabet of Christian names, but when we consider that the Spaniards and Portuguese stand alone among European nations in respect to the importance they pay to the Christian name, and remember further that authors and others are often alluded to by their Christian names alone, we shall see a valid reason for the plan. Another point that should not be forgotten is the number of Spanish authors who have belonged to religious orders, and are never known by their surnames. This arrangement, however, necessitates a full index of surnames, and Antonio has given one which was highly praised by both Baillet and Bayle, two men who were well able to form an opinion.

When Baillet, the learned author of the *Jugemens des Savans,* was appointed by M. de Lamoignon, keeper of the exquisite library collected by that nobleman, he set to work to compile an index of the contents of all the books contained in it, and this he is said to have completed in August, 1682. After this date, however, the Index continued to grow, and it extended to thirty-two folio volumes, all written by Baillet's own hand. It is clear from this that that eminent bibliographer lived two hundred years before his time. How highly would his labours be appreciated now were he Director of the Index Society.

The great Bayle, as might be expected from his omnivorous literary appetite, held the vocation of the Index-maker in high esteem. He quotes with approval Antonio's remark respecting the author of a book being the proper person to index it, but he adds with justice that it is not every author who is capable of making an index, a doctrine also preached by Le Clerc. Bayle adds, "Authors refer to others the pains of making alphabetical Indexes; and it must be owned, that those gentlemen who are not patient of labour, and whose talent consists only in the fire and vivacity of imagination, had much better let others make the Index to their works." To show the need of judgment in this department of literary labour, Bayle refers to the drawer-up of the Index to Dalechamp's Athenæus, "who says that Euripides lost in one day his wife, two sons, and a daughter, and refers us to page 60, where nothing like this is found; but we find in page 61 that Euripides, going to Icaria, wrote an epigram on a disaster that happened at a peasant's house, where a woman, with her two sons and a daughter, died by eating of mushrooms." In order to guard against such blunders, Bayle proposed that certain directions should be drawn up for the guidance of the compilers of indexes, which have justly been called the soul of books.[1]

If we examine the indexes to old books, we shall certainly find ample reason for the belief that in former centuries authors

[1] "M. Bochart . . . . me prioit surtout d'y faire [i.e. his Diogenes Laertius] un *Index,* étant, disoit-il, l'âme des gros livres."—*Menagiana,* Paris, 1729, tome i. p. 75.

more frequently had a hand in the production of the indexes to
their books than they have in the present day.   Leigh Hunt,
in a pleasant paper written for the *Indicator*, says : "Index
making has been held to be the driest as well as lowest species
of writing.   We shall not dispute the humbleness of it ; but
since we have had to make an index ourselves we have discovered
that the task need not be so very dry.   Calling to mind indexes
in general, we found them presenting us a variety of pleasant
memories and contrasts."   He then praises the Indexes to the
Tatler and Spectator, and adds : "Our index seemed the poorest
and most second-hand thing in the world after theirs : but let
any one read theirs and then call an index a dry thing if he can.
As there 'is a soul of goodness in things evil,' so there is a soul
of humour in things dry, and in things dry by profession."
He then quotes from Cotton's Montaigne and Sandys's Ovid.
From the latter he gives the following specimens :

> "Dwarfes, an Italian dwarfe carried about in a parrot's cage, p. 113.
> Eccho at Twilleries in Paris, heard to repeat a verse without failing in
> one syllable, p. 58.
> Ship of the Tyrrhenians miraculously stuck fast in the sea, p. 63.
> A Historie of a British ship stuck fast in the deepe sea by witchcraft :
> for which twentie five witches were executed, *ibid.*"

The index to Cotton's translation of Montaigne's Essays
(which was added to the book after Cotton's death) is full of
quaint entries ; for instance, these four will give some idea of
the others :

> "Books, immortal children.
> Children abandon'd to the care and government of their fathers !
> Ears, dangerous instruments.
> Glosses upon books augment doubts."

Swift prefixed an amusing analytical Table to his 'Tale of a
Tub,' and the first edition of Shenstone's burlesque poem, the
Schoolmistress, contains a ludicrous index or table of contents,
which the poet added "purely to show fools that I am in jest."
In subsequent editions this table was suppressed, but Disraeli
reprinted it in his *Curiosities of Literature*.   It is too long to
quote entire here, and a specimen will be sufficient to show its
scope :

"A circumstance in the situation of mansion of early discipline, discovering the surprising influence of the connection of ideas.

Some peculiarities indicative of a country school, with a short sketch of the sovereign presiding over it.

Some account of her night-cap, apron and a tremendous description of her birchen sceptre.

The secret connection between whipping and rising in the world, with a view as it were, through a perspective, of the same little folk in the higher posts and reputation."

This 'ludicrous index' very probably gave Southey a hint which he worked out in the headings for chapters to his *Doctor*.

This seems to be the proper place to mention the practice that arose in the last century of drawing up indexes of sentiments and opinions as opposed to facts. Such indexes required a special skill in the indexer, who was usually the original author. There is a curious poetical index to the Iliad in Pope's Homer, referring to all the places in which similes are used. Dr. Johnson was very anxious that Richardson should produce such an index to his novels. In the *Correspondence of Samuel Richardson* (vol. v. p. 282), is a letter from the lexicographer to the novelist to the following effect : "I wish you would add an *index rerum*, that when the reader recollects any incident, he may easily find it, which at present he cannot do, unless he knows in which volume it is told; for Clarissa is not a performance to be read with eagerness, and laid aside for ever; but will be occasionally consulted by the busy, the aged and the studious; and therefore I beg that this edition, by which I suppose posterity is to abide, may want nothing that can facilitate its use." At the end of each volume of "Clarissa" Richardson added a sort of table of all the passages best worth remembering, and as he was the judge, it naturally extended to a considerable length. In September, 1753, Johnson again wrote to Richardson, suggesting the propriety of making an index to his three works, but he added: "While I am writing an objection arises ; such an index to the three would look like the preclusion of a fourth, to which I will never contribute ; for if I cannot benefit mankind I hope never to injure them." Richardson took the hint of his distinguished friend, and in 1755 appeared a volume of 410 pages, entitled "A Collection of the moral and instructive Sentiments, Maxims, Cautions and Reflexions contained in the

Histories of Pamela, Clarissa and Sir Charles Grandison, digested under proper heads." The production of this book was a labour of love to its author, who, moreover, was skilled in the mechanical work of indexing, and in the early part of his career had filled up his leisure hours by compiling indexes for the booksellers and writing prefaces and dedications.

The high praise given by Leigh Hunt to Steele's indexes has already been noted, and a casual reference to the index of the *Tatler* will show the justice of the remark : " As grapes ready to burst with wine issue out of the most stony places, like jolly fellows bringing burgundy out of a cellar, so an Index like the Tatler's often gives us a taste of the quintessence of his humour." The very title gives good promise of what is to follow : " A faithful Index of the dull as well as the ingenious passages in the Tatler." Here are a few entries chosen at random :

Vol. 1. Bachelor's scheme to govern a wife.
　　　　Knaves proved fools.
Vol. 2. Dead men, who.
　　　　Dead persons heard, judged and censured.
　　　　———— allegations laid against them, their pleas.
　　　　Love letters before and after marriage, found in a grave.
　　　　Mathematical sieve to sift impertinences in writing and discourse.
Vol. 4. Blockheads apt to admire one another.

In 1757 "A General Index to the Spectators, Tatlers and Guardians" was published, and in 1760 the same work was reissued with a new title-page. Certain blots in the original indexes were here corrected, and the following explanation made in the preface : " Notwithstanding the learning and care of the compilers of the first Indexes to these volumes, some slight inaccuracies have passed, and where observed they are altered. Few readers who desire to know Mr. Bickerstaff's opinion of the Comedy called the Country Wife, or the character of Mrs. Bickerstaff as an actress, would consult the Index. under the word *Acts*."

Michael Maittaire, the bibliographer, prided himself on his talent for index-making, which he exhibited in his editions of the classics, and in his '.Annales Typographici.' William

Bowyer, the learned printer, made the excellent Index to William Clarke's "Connexion of the Roman, Saxon and English Coins" (1767), which greatly pleased the author, who wrote to Bowyer, "Of all your talents you are a most amazing man at Indexes. What a flag, too, do you hang out at the stern! You must certainly persuade people that the book overflows with matter, which (to speak the truth) is but thinly spread. But I know all this is fair in trade, and you have a right to expect that the publick should purchase freely when you reduce the whole book into an epitome for their benefit ; I shall read the Index with pleasure." [1] Bowyer's biographer, John Nichols, to whom we owe the *Literary Anecdotes of the Eighteenth Century*, and the *Illustrations of Literary History*, two books treasured by all lovers of bibliography, was an Indexer of merit, and his son and grandson followed in his footsteps. The memory of Dr. Maty has often been blessed by consulters of the *Philosophical Transactions*, who find great help in his copious Index to the first seventy volumes of that work.

Samuel Ayscough was another industrious index-maker who deserves especial mention. He compiled indexes for the Monthly Review, the British Critic, and the Gentleman's Magazine. His Index to Shakespeare (1790) was a work of great labour and high utility, followed, in 1804, by Francis Twiss's *Verbal Index*, and quite superseded by Mrs. Cowden Clarke's complete Concordance (1844). It is under the heading of Ayscough, in his Dictionary of Authors, that Allibone has gathered together an interesting collection of quotations on the subject of indexes.

The industrious E. H. Barker took the greatest pleasure in making the Index to his edition of Stephens's Thesaurus (which was so mauled in the 'Quarterly' by Bishop Blomfield), and when a friend condoled with him on the bore of making the index, which had occupied three years in the composing and printing, Mr. Barker observed that they were the happiest years of his life, for he had thus read again and again the *Thesaurus*, which he should not otherwise have done.

The name of the great historian Macaulay will appropriately

---

[1] Nichols's Literary Anecdotes, vol. iii. p. 46.

close this list of eminent indexers. At the age of fifteen he wrote a letter to Hannah More, which ends with these words : " To add to the list, my dear madam, you will soon see a work of mine in print. Do not be frightened ; it is only the Index to the thirteenth volume of the *Christian Observer*, which I have had the honour of composing. Index-making, though the lowest, is not the most useless round in the ladder of literature ; and I pride myself upon being able to say that there are many readers of the *Christian Observer* who could do without Walter Scott's works, but not without those of, my dear madam, your affectionate friend, THOMAS B. MACAULAY." Macaulay in after-life used a contemptuous expression when he was describing the appearance of the lowest grade in the literary profession. My friend Mr. Campkin, a veteran Indexer, quotes this description in the preface to one of his valuable Indexes—that to the twenty-five volumes of the *Sussex Archæological Collections*—" The compilation of Indexes will always, and naturally so, be regarded as a humble art : 'index-makers in ragged coats of frieze' are classed by Lord Macaulay as the very lowest of the frequenters of the coffee-houses of the Dryden and Swift era. Yet ''tis my vocation, Hal,' and into very pleasant companionship it has sometimes brought me, and if in this probably the last of my twenty-five years' labours in this direction, I have succeeded in furnishing a fairly practicable key to a valuable set of volumes, my frieze coat, how tattered soever signifieth not, will continue to hang upon my shoulders not uncomfortably." Mr. Campkin is quite right as to the estimation in which the indexer is held, but I think he should not allow that such estimation is natural. The art that requires thought and some power of analysis should in justice be rated higher than this, and if the Index-makers did such good work as we frequently find in the books of the seventeenth and eighteenth centuries, the discredit of the ragged coats would rightly belong to their employers and not to themselves. Macaulay probably had Swift's *Account of the Condition of Edmund Curll* in his mind when he alluded to the low estate of the Index-maker. In this satire there are certain " Instructions to a Porter how to find Mr. Curll's authors," few of whom are in sufficiently easy circumstances to allow of the renting a garret each for himself—"At the laundress's at the Hole in the Wall in Cursitor's Alley up three pair of stairs, the author of my Church history—you may also speak to the gentleman who lies by him in the flock bed, my index maker."

No account of the history of indexing would be complete without special and honourable mention of two literary men who have persistently pointed out on all occasions the urgent need of Indexes. One of these is an Englishman and the other an American. Mr. Thoms, as editor of the "*Notes and Queries*," must constantly have felt the want of these helps to research, and he seldom allowed a volume of his journal to pass without inserting something regarding them. He did more however, for he issued a General Index to each series as it was completed. Dr. Allibone, throughout his *Dictionary of English and American Authors*, has lost no opportunity of saying something to the purpose on his favourite subject. As already remarked, he printed at the beginning of the first volume of his great work a most interesting series of quotations relating to Indexes and on the very last page of his third and last volume he returned to the subject in bidding farewell to his readers.

Mr. Markland is the authority for the declaration by the Roxburghe Club that "the omission of an Index when essential should be an indictable offence."[1] Carlyle denounces the putters forth of indexless books; and Baynes, the author of the *Archæological Epistle to Dean Milles* (which is usually attributed to Mason), concocted a terrible curse against such evil-doers. The reporter was the learned Francis Douce, who said to Mr. Thoms, "Sir, my friend John Baynes used to say that the man who published a book without an index ought to be damned ten miles beyond Hell, where the Devil could not get for stinging nettles."[2]

Lord Campbell proposed that any author who published a book without an Index should be deprived of the benefits of the Copyright Act, and the Hon. Horace Binney, LL.D., a distinguished American lawyer, held the same views, and

---

[1] Notes and Queries, 2nd series, vol. vii. p. 469.
[2] Notes and Queries, 5th series, vol. viii. p. 87.

would have condemned the culprit to the same punishment. Those, however, who hold the justest theories sometimes fail in practice; thus Lord Campbell had to acknowledge that he had himself sinned before the year 1857; and the deficiencies of the forty Indexes to Allibone's Dictionary are pointed out in a paper read before the Conference of Librarians in October, 1877.[1] These are the words written by Lord Campbell in the preface to the first volume of his *Lives of the Chief Justices* (1857)—"I have only further to express my satisfaction in thinking that a heavy weight is now to be removed from my conscience. So essential did I consider an Index to be to every book, that I proposed to bring a Bill into Parliament to deprive an author who publishes a book without an Index of the privilege of copyright; and moreover to subject him for his offence to a pecuniary penalty. Yet from difficulties started by my printers, my own books have hitherto been without an Index. But I am happy to announce that a learned friend at the bar, on whose accuracy I can place entire reliance, has kindly prepared a copious Index which will be appended to this work, and another for the new stereotyped edition of the Lives of the Chancellors."

In tracing the history of Index-making we have seen that the value of a full Index was early realized; but when authors ceased to make their own indexes, neglect was the consequence, and during the early part of the present century this period of neglect was probably the most complete. Towards the formation of general Indexes little had been done until late years, although we have seen that Baillet set himself to such work. Of special Indexes we should naturally expect that one to the Bible would be the first attempted, and such was the case. The first Concordance was compiled by Hugo de St. Caro, in 1247, and five hundred monks are said to have been employed upon it. The first English concordance to any part of the Scriptures was of the New Testament, and printed by Thomas Gybson in 1536. That to the entire Bible was made by John Marbeck, and published at London by Grafton in 1550.[2] Previously to the publication of this valuable work

[1] See Transactions of the Conference, p. 88.
[2] For full title see p. 75.

Marbeck was shut up in the Marshalsea, but when Henry VIII. pardoned him he told the Bishops that Marbeck had employed his time much better than they had theirs. Nearly two centuries later Alexander Cruden published his great work, which still continues to be the standard Concordance.

In 1545 an alphabetical Collection of the most elegant words and phrases used by Boccaccio was compiled by Francis Alunno, and published in *Le Ricchezze della Lingua volgare.* Verbal Indexes to the ancient classics afterwards became common, and in 1662 the celebrated *Gradus ad Parnassum* first appeared under the title of "Epithetorum et Synonymorum Thesaurus" (Paris). It is attributed to Chatillon, and was reprinted by Paul Aler, a German Jesuit, as the *Gradus.*[1]

The lawyers can claim the honour of being the first class to realize the absolute need of Indexes, and the Digests produced by them are admirable works, but the greatest lawyers still point out how much there is to be done. Sir Henry Thring has drawn up some masterly instructions for an Index to the Statute Law, which is to be considered as a step towards a code. These instructions conclude with the following weighty words—"Let no man imagine that the construction of an index to the Statute Law is a mere piece of mechanical drudgery, unworthy of the energy and ability of an accomplished lawyer. Next to codification the most difficult task that can be accomplished is to prepare a detailed plan for a code, as distinct from the easy task of devising a theoretical system of codification. Now the preparation of an index, such as has been suggested in the above instructions, is the preparation of a detailed plan for a code. Each effec-

---

[1] I searched in vain for the date of the first edition of the *Gradus,* until I was so fortunate as to find it in the valuable article on "Dictionaries" in the new edition of the *Encyclopædia Britannica.* Little information was to be obtained from the British Museum Catalogue, owing to the complicated arrangement of the anonymous books. I looked into the new General Catalogue under the heading *Parnassus,* where the book should have been entered according to the rules, and there was only one edition of the present century. I then turned to *Gradus,* and there was a reference to an edition by Valpy. I knew that there must be some earlier edition, so I went to the old General Catalogue and there I at once found others an "editio novissima" (Coloniæ Agrippinæ, 1687). When the book was in my hands I noticed that it was marked to be catalogued under the heading of "Dictionaries," where I venture to think few would look for it. This experience is related here as a good illustration of the inconvenience of classification in an Alphabetical Catalogue.

tive title is, in effect, a plan for the codification of the legal
subject-matter grouped under that title, and the whole index,
if completed, would be a summary of a code arranged in
alphabetical order." [1]

That this question of digesting the law is to be considered
as one that should interest all classes of Englishmen, and not
the lawyer only, may be seen from an article in the *Nineteenth
Century* (September, 1877), on the "Improvement of the Law by
private enterprise," by Sir James Fitzjames Stephen, who has
done so much towards a complete digest of the law. He writes:
" I have long believed that the law might by proper means be
relieved of this extreme obscurity and intricacy, and might be
displayed in its true light as a subject of study of the deepest
possible interest, not only to every one who takes an interest in
politics or ethics, or in the application of logic and metaphysics
to those subjects.   In short, I think that nothing but the re-
arrangement and condensation of the vast masses of matter
contained in our law libraries is required, in order to add to
human knowledge what would be practically a new department
of the highest and most permanent interest.   Law holds in
suspension both the logic and the ethics, which are, in fact,
recognized by men of business and men of the world as the
standards by which the practice of common life ought to be
regulated, and by which men ought to form their opinions in
all their most important temporal affairs.   It would be a far
greater service to mankind than many people would suppose to
have these standards clearly defined and brought within the
reach of every one who cared to study them."   The following
remarks will apply with equal force to a more general and
universal index than that of the law : " The preparation of a
digest either of the whole or of any branch of the law is work
of a very peculiar kind.   It is one of the very few literary
undertakings in which a number of persons can really and
effectively work together.   Any given subject may, it is true,
be dealt with in a variety of different ways; but when the
general scheme, according to which it is to be treated, has been
determined on, when the skeleton of the book has been drawn

---

[1] These instructions, with specimens of the proposed Index, are printed in the
Law Magazine for August, 1877, 4th series, vol. 8, p. 491.

out, plenty of persons might be found to do the work of filling up the details, *though that work is very far from being easy or a matter of routine.*"

The value of analytical or index work is set in a very strong light by an observation of Sir James Stephen, respecting the early digesters of the law. The origin of English law is to be found in the Year Books and other series of old Reports, which, from the language used in them, and the black-letter printing, with its contractions, etc., are practically inaccessible. Coke and others who reduced these books into form are, in consequence, treated as ultimate authorities, although the almost worshipped Coke is said by Sir James to be " one of the most confused, pedantic and inaccurate of men."

Parliament has long recognized the fact that the preparation of indexes to their journals is a department of work upon which large sums of money may be advantageously spent. In 1778 a total of £12,900 was voted for Indexes to the Journals of the House of Commons. The items were as follows: To Mr. Edward Moore, £6400 as a final compensation for thirteen years' labour; Rev. Mr. Forster, £3000 for nine years' labour; Rev. Dr. Roger Flaxman, £3000 for nine years' labour; and £500 to Mr. Cunningham.

But one of the grandest and most useful applications of index-making is to be found in the series of Calendars of State Papers, issued under the sanction of the Master of the Rolls, which have made available to all a mass of historical material previously hardly appreciated by the few.

Scientific men have found by bitter experience that, unless they have the assistance of indexes, they must spend years in studying the bibliography of their subject, if they would avoid doing again what has already been done. It has so long been the popular belief that the work of indexing may properly be deputed to the harmless drudge, whose industry is his chief merit, that it is no ordinary gratification to be able to point to the great physiologist Haller as one who, knowing that genius must have its toils, and finding that no such works had been produced, stepped aside from his grander labours to compile bibliographies of the science his talents adorned. In the words of Johnson, index-making has been supposed to be " a task that requires neither the light of learning nor the activity of genius, but may be successfully performed without any higher quality than that of bearing burthens with dull patience, and beating the track of the alphabet with sluggish resolution."[1] That Albert von Haller did not hold this disgraceful doctrine his *Bibliotheca Botanica* (1771), his *Bibliotheca Anatomica* (1774–77), his *Bibliotheca Chirurgica* (1774–75) and his *Bibliotheca Medicinæ practicæ* (1776–78) amply prove.

We find in these bibliographies a large proportion of University Theses and Inaugural Dissertations, a form of publication which was in considerable favour before the more general issue of journals and transactions of Societies. When these latter became numerous, the need of some key to their hidden contents was greatly felt, and a large unoccupied field for indexing was here discovered. In 1800 Reuss commenced at Gottingen the publication of his *Repertorium Commentationum a Societatibus Literariis editarum*, which was continued for twenty years, and completed in sixteen quarto volumes. The contents are arranged and classified according to the chief divisions of knowledge. The well-known publisher Engelmann, of Leipzig, is deserving of the greatest credit for his extensive series of special Bibliographies. That of Zoology, by Dr. Carus (1861), is one of the most important of these publications, and to a great extent superseded the *Bibliographia Zoologiæ* of Agassiz, which was published by the Ray Society (1848–54). These works helped to make apparent to all the want which they did not completely supply. In 1857 the Royal Society undertook the preparation of a Catalogue of Scientific Papers in British and Foreign Journals and Transactions, from the commencement of the present century. This was a vast work, and necessarily occupied a considerable time in preparation. When it was thought advisable to commence printing, the limit of date for the papers was fixed at 1863. In 1867 the first volume was published, and each succeeding year a double-columned quarto volume, of about 1000 pages, appeared until 1872, when the Alphabet of Authors was completed in the sixth volume. A supplement for the years 1864–73 is in

---

[1] *Plan of an English Dictionary.*

course of publication. The value of the Catalogue is grate-
fully acknowledged on all hands, and it has now become so
indispensable that every consulter must marvel how scientific
men managed to get on without it.   Medical men, however,
complain that medical and surgical papers have been passed
over, and Dr. J. S. Billings, Librarian of the U.S. National
Medical Library, is attempting to do for these departments
what has already been done for general science.   In 1876 was
printed a *Specimen Fasciculus of a Catalogue of the National
Medical Library under the direction of the Surgeon General of the
U.S. Army at Washington,* and in the May number (1878) of
the *Library Journal* is an article by Dr. Billings on the *National
Catalogue of Medical Literature* to contain references to papers
in all the Medical Journals.   It is estimated that the Subject
Catalogue would occupy about seven volumes of one thousand
pages each, and the Authors' Catalogue about three volumes
extra.   The question of printing this great work is now before
Congress, and Dr. Billings puts the following query to be
answered by Librarians and others : " What is the value of
such an index to the people of the United States as compared
with an expedition to the North Pole, five miles of subsidized
railway, one company of cavalry, or a small post office building ? "

There cannot be two opinions as to the importance of such a
publication, not only to the United States but to the world.
At present the Indexes to the Catalogues of the Libraries of
the College of Surgeons and the Royal Medical and Chirurgical
Society serve the purpose of a special bibliography of medical
literature, but they only refer to books and not to the contents
of those books.

Every year new societies and new journals are started in
various parts of the world, so that it becomes daily more difficult for workers to keep themselves *au courant* with the work
of others.   To obviate this difficulty the Zoologists started in
1864 an annual Record of their science, and the Geologists
followed suit in 1874.   The Chemists, in 1871, adopted the
still more useful plan of a monthly *resume* of chemical papers,
and with each number of the *Journal of the Chemical Society*
is published a series of abstracts of papers in foreign journals.

The year's numbers, completed with a full index, form an annual Record. Several foreign journals are also published with the main object of giving abstracts of books and papers published on their respective subjects, such for instance as the various German "Centralblatt." A monthly part of the *Polybiblon : Revue Bibliographique Universelle*, is specially devoted to summaries of the contents of various French and Foreign periodicals. In America the contents of current periodicals are recorded in "The Library Table" and in "The American Bookseller." A classified Index of the Proceedings of the Learned Societies and the contents of the principal magazines and reviews is announced as a feature of the newly-started English Journal—"The Book-Analyst and Library Guide." On all sides there is evidence of the rapid growth of a taste for bibliographical research. Scientific journals and transactions now contain papers full of bibliographical details, which a few years ago would not have been considered suitable for publication in immediate proximity to original scientific papers; and this is not to be wondered at, for the many questions of priority that constantly arise can only be settled by the correct statement of the date of publication. The British Association publish reports on the history of science, which are made up of accurate lists of books and papers. The *Philosophical Magazine* [1] contains an account of early Books on Logarithms, by Mr. J. W. L. Glaisher, F.R.S. ; the *Memoirs of the Royal Astronomical Society* [2] has a Chronology of Star Catalogues, by Mr. E. B. Knobel ; the *Transactions of the Connecticut Academy*, [3] a list of writings relating to the method of least squares, with historical and critical notes by Mansfield Merriman ; and the *Annals of the Lyceum of Natural History of New York*, "Outlines of a Bibliography of the History of Chemistry," [4] and Index to the Literature of Manganese, 1596–1874, [5] both by H. Carrington Bolton, Ph.D.

Prof. J. Plateau, the distinguished physicist, is publishing by sections, a "Bibliographie Analytique des principaux phé-nomènes subjectifs de la Vision," in the Memoirs of the Brussels Academy. Mr. Edward S. Holden, of the Wash-

[1] Fourth series, vol. 44.   [2] Vol. 43, p. 1.   [3] Vol. 4, p. 151.   [4] Vol. 10.   [5] Vol. 11.

ington Naval Observatory, has prepared a valuable "Index Catalogue of Books and Memoirs relating to Nebulæ and Clusters," which was published in 1871 by the Smithsonian Institution, to whom we owe so much good work in this direction; and in 1878 the same gentleman's "Index Catalogue of Books and Memoirs on the Transits of Mercury " was issued as No. 1 of the "Bibliographical Contributions (Library of Harvard University)," edited by Justin Winsor. Monographs are now seldom published without some index of the bibliography of the subject. Dr. Copland was one of the first to make the notice of the literature of all topics treated a special feature in his *Dictionary of Practical Medicine*. Many scientific books on special subjects are in fact indexes; thus Morris's *Catalogue of British Fossils* (2nd ed. 1854); Bigsby's *Thesaurus Siluricus* (1868); and the same veteran geologist's *Thesaurus Devonico-Carboniferus* (1878), are tables of fossils with references to places where descriptions will be found. This is the index work which is acknowledged on all hands to be of the greatest value in the saving of the student's time.

In passing from the consideration of Indexes of science to those of general literature, the place of honour must be given to Mr. Poole's *Index of Periodical Literature*. The author gave an interesting account of the origin of his work at the Conference of Librarians held in London (October, 1877). When Librarian at Yale College, Mr. Poole made a list of the articles in the journals in the Library for his own private use. The assistance he was thus able to give to readers was highly appreciated, and he was asked to allow the list to be printed for the benefit of others. This first edition appeared in 1848, and a greatly enlarged edition followed in 1853. The second edition is out of print, and a new one is in preparation, under the superintendence of the compiler, but with the co-operation of librarians both in America and Great Britain. Mr. Poole said that he had not seen a copy of his first edition for twenty years until he saw it on the shelves of the Reading Room of the British Museum. The nearest approach to a general Index in existence is the useful Catalogue of Subjects which forms the third and fourth volumes of Watt's *Bibliotheca Britannica*. The Index attached to Darling's

Cyclopædia has several useful features, but the work was never finished. One of the completest Catalogues ever published is that of the Library of the London Institution. It is classified and has an Index of Authors. It was not usual to attach an Index of Subjects to a Catalogue of Authors until late years, and that to the Athenæum Library (1852) is an early specimen. The New York State Library Catalogue, 1856, has an Index, as have those of the Medical and Chirurgical Library (1860) and the London Library (1865 and 1875). That appended to the Catalogue of the Manchester Free Library (1864) is more a short list of titles than an Index. In any notice of this kind the valuable Indexes to the various collections of MSS. in the British Museum must not be omitted, nor Mr. Sampson Low's Index to the British Catalogue of Books (1858), which was compiled by Dr. Crestadoro, Librarian of the Manchester Free Library. Indexes to series of Journals have naturally been frequent, but it was a novelty when the Parker Society published a general Index to their separate publications—a work of the greatest utility which the Camden Society propose to emulate.

That the interest felt in Index work is pretty generally spread abroad, may be guessed by a paragraph that went the round of the papers a few months ago, to the effect that an Index or 'Repertorium' of the contents of all the German military magazines and periodicals, which have been published during the last sixteen years, has been lately printed at Berlin, which it is supposed will be of great value to every student of military art, and even to the more general reader.

The various matters treated of in the previous pages, go to prove the existence of a revived interest in the value of Indexes, and seem naturally to lead up to a notice of the formation of the Index Society. The founders lay no claim to originality of conception; but they think that the widespread feeling of the need of some such organization, which has been frequently expressed, will insure the success of the Society.

In 1854 an announcement was made in the "Notes and Queries"[1] of the projected formation of a "Society for the

Formation of a General Literary Index." In the second series (vol. i. p. 486), the late Mr. Thomas Jones, who signed himself Bibliothecar. Chetham., commenced a series of articles, which he continued for several years, as a contribution to this General Index; but nothing more was heard of the Society. Inquiries were made in various numbers of the *Notes and Queries* respecting its formation, but no response was made. In 1870 a contributor to the same periodical, signing himself A. H., proposed the formation of a staff of Index compilers. In 1874 Prof. Stanley Jevons published his *Principles of Science.* In the chapter on Classification, he enlarges on the value of Indexes, and adds : "The time will perhaps come when our views upon this subject will be extended, and either Government or some public society will undertake the systematic cataloguing and indexing of masses of historical and scientific information, which are now almost closed against inquiry " (1st ed. vol. ii. p. 405 ; 2nd. ed. p. 718).

In the following year Mr. Edward Solly and the writer of these pages, without having seen this passage, consulted as to the possibility of starting an Index Society, but postponed the actual carrying out of their scheme for a time. In July, 1875, Mr. J. Ashton Cross argued in a pamphlet, that a Universal Index might be formed by co-operation through a clearing-house, and would pay if published in separate parts. In September, 1877, some letters were printed in the *Pall Mall Gazette* by one who signed himself 'A Lover of Indexes,' in which the foundation of an Index Society was strongly urged. In October, 1877, Mr. Cross read a paper before the Conference of Librarians, which was a revival of the scheme previously suggested. All these movements in different quarters proved that the train was widely spread, and only needed the lighting spark to make itself apparent; or, to use another metaphor, the volunteers were ready for their work, and only waited for the bugle call, and this was given in the *Athenæum* for October 13, 1877, in a report of the Conference of Librarians written by Mr. Robert Harrison. There we read : "Could not a permanent Index Society be founded with the support of voluntary contributions of money as well as of subject matter ? In this way a regular staff could be set to work, under competent direction, and could be kept steadily at work until its performances became so generally known and so useful as to enable it to stand alone and be self-supporting. Many readers would readily jot down the name of any new subject they meet with in the book before them, and the page on which it occurs, and forward their notes to be sorted and arranged by any Society that would undertake the work."

The following number of the *Athenæum* contained letters in approval of the suggestion from Mr. G. Laurence Gomme and from Professor Justin Winsor, of Harvard, who wrote: "We have been in America striving for years to get some organized body to undertake this very work." In the number for October 27, it was announced that steps were being taken for the formation of the Society, and the editor complained that he had been overwhelmed with letters on the subject for which he could not find space.

In closing this general notice of Index work, and before passing on to the consideration of the various modes of indexing, it will perhaps be well to offer some answer to the question—What can such a Society do? We have seen how highly a good Index is appreciated by workers, but it does not need much argument to prove how few such there are, and how many more are wanted. It has been said that a big book is a great evil, and so it is until it receives an Index, and then it becomes a great good. Prof. De Morgan, who treated Bibliography in a more interesting manner than many authors treat lighter subjects, says, when referring to Samuel Jeake's "Arithmetick surveighed and reviewed," (1696) in his *Arithmetical Books*—"Those who know the value of a large book with a good index will pick this one up when they can." Mr. Jeake published his work in a folio volume, the size and weight of which made De Morgan suggest the possibility that the author thought arithmetic was a branch of controversial divinity. In spite of this he singles it out for praise on account of the value of the information it contains and the fullness of the references to this information. I think we see in various directions evidence of an awakening of interest in Index work, but this interest wants fostering, and if book-buyers will agree to give the preference to well-indexed books, the publishers will soon be eager to supply the want so generally recognized. We may then hope to see the time when it will be as rare to find a book without an Index as without a title-page. The Library Association of the United Kingdom have set a good example by issuing the Report of the Conference of Librarians, 1877, with an elaborate Index to its varied contents, which has been much appreciated, and does great credit to Mr. Tedder who compiled it.

To direct public attention to a neglected subject is one of the main objects of the Index Society; but although Indexes to new books may be demanded from publishers, it is hardly to be expected that these merchants in literature will index books of the past. There are a large number of standard works to which students must frequently refer, which are a source of constant irritation from the difficulty of finding what is required in their voluminous pages. The county and local histories, in the possession of which England is so rich, rank high in the list of these—a list which would also contain the Standard Historical Collections, such as those of Rushworth, and Nalson, the Harleian Miscellany, Somers' Tracts, Ellis's Original Letters, and many other books that it is needless to enumerate here.[1] To this department the Society will devote special attention. In all cases a book that may be considered as *the* authority upon a given subject will have the preference, so that the Indexes may serve as complete guides to the various topics. In many instances the works of standard authors will be indexed as a whole, and in this way Indexes to particular books or authors will often be Subject Indexes as well. With these and Subject Indexes referring to Books and Papers in British and Foreign Journals and Transactions, it is hoped that in a few years the Society will have accumulated and published a series of books that will be of real service to all classes of readers.

---

[1] "The Rushworths, Whitlockes, Nalsons, Thurloes; enormous folios, these and many others have been printed, and some of them again printed, but never yet edited,—edited as you edit wagon-loads of broken bricks and dry mortar simply by tumbling up the wagon! Not one of those monstrous old volumes has so much as an available Index. It is the general rule of editing on this matter. If your editor correct the press, it is an honourable distinction."—*Carlyle's Introduction to Cromwell's Letters and Speeches.*

Much that would otherwise be neglected may be done by a public society, but to attack with effect the mass of work waiting to be undertaken, it is necessary that we should receive a hearty support. It is to the interest of subscribers to make the objects of the Society widely known, and otherwise to help it, because the more numerous the subscribers the larger will be the return that each subscriber will get for his subscription, and the larger the plot of the great field that can be put under cultivation. It is expected that the work of the Society will be largely extended when they acquire funds that will enable them to open an office which shall contain a library of indexes, and in which can be placed the General Reference Index.

I have heard two objections brought against the scheme of the Society :

1. That it is needless to urge the compilation of indexes, because every worker worthy of the name makes his own. This, however, is just the loss of power that the Society wish to prevent. Now the same work is often done over and over again, and the MSS. are only saved from the waste-paper basket by the merest chance, to be again lost among a heap of other papers. There are, doubtless, many valuable indexes lying hidden and unknown, and it will be our object to draw them if possible to the light.

2. That the General Index is an impossibility, and that to attempt its preparation is a waste of time. Those who hold this opinion have not sufficient faith in the simplicity and usefulness of the alphabet. Every one has notes and references of some kind, which are useless if kept unarranged, but if sorted into alphabetical order become valuable. The object of the General Index is just this, that anything, however disconnected, can be placed there, and much that would otherwise be lost will there find a resting place. Always growing and never pretending to be complete, the Index will be useful to all, and its consulters will be sure to find something worth their trouble if not all they may require.

The objects of the Society are national in their importance, and as such they have been acknowledged by one who has given one hundred guineas to help in their attainment. With more such gifts how much might be done by the Society.

Having dwelt in the previous pages upon some of the chief points in the history of Indexing, we will now pass on to the consideration of the practical part of the subject. The unwise seem to be of opinion that any fool can index, but we have already seen that the wise think differently. The remarks with which Dr. Johnson opens the preface to his English Dictionary may well be applied to the Indexer: "It is the fate of those who toil at the lower employments of life to be rather driven by the fear of evil, than attracted by the prospect of good; to be exposed to censure, without hope of praise; to be disgraced by miscarriage, or punished for neglect, where success would have been without applause, and diligence without reward. Among these unhappy mortals is the writer of dictionaries; whom mankind have considered, not as the pupil, but the slave of science, the pioneer of literature, doomed only to remove rubbish and clear obstructions from the paths through which Learning and Genius press forward to conquest and glory, without bestowing a smile on the humble drudge that facilitates their progress. Every other author may aspire to praise; the lexicographer can only hope to escape reproach, and even this negative recompence has been yet granted to very few." This dishonouring estimate has received many rude shocks, and it should be our aim to crush it entirely out of existence.

In order to give some appearance of system to what might otherwise be considered as mere desultory remarks, I propose to arrange the following notes under the three heads of I. Compilation; II. Arrangement; III. Printing.

I.

In the Instructions for an Index to the Statute Law, by Sir Henry Thring,[1] already referred to, we find the following clear definitions which will serve to open this portion of our case :—

"The basis of an index to a book of the ordinary kind is a series of titles or catch-words arranged in alphabetical order and indicative of the main topics treated of in the book."

"The object of an index is to indicate the place in a book or collection

[1] Law Magazine, August, 1877.

of books in which particular information is to be found. Such an index is perfect in proportion as it is concise in expression, whilst exhaustive in its indication of every important topic of the subject to which it is an index."

The question naturally arises—how is the work to be set about ? In the Special Report on the Public Libraries of the United States of America, Part I, 1876 (pp. 727–732), is an article on "Book Indexes" by F. B. Perkins, which contains some rather elementary instruction as to writing, cutting up, and pasting, but in these matters of detail the best way of proceeding will always be the way that the indexer feels that he can work best. Some choose to write their Index straight on in the order of the book itself, on sheets of paper which are afterwards cut up, sorted, and pasted; others prefer to use slips of paper and to write one entry on each slip; a third class will make their entries at once into an alphabetical book, or better still on loose sheets of paper placed in a portfolio lettered in alphabetical order. By this means the indexer sees his work grow under his hands. Whatever system however is adopted, it is well to bear in mind that the indexer should obtain some knowledge of the book he is about to Index before he commences his work. The following remarks by Sir H. Thring may be applied more generally than to the law—"A complete knowledge of the whole *law* is required before he begins to make the index, for until he can look down on the entire field of law before him, he cannot possibly judge of the proper arrangement of the headings, or of the relative importance of the various provisions."

During his work the Indexer must constantly ask himself what it is for which the consulter is likely to seek. The author frequently uses periphrases to escape from the repetition of the same fact in the same form, but these periphrases will give little information when inserted as headings in an Index, and it is in this point of selecting the best catchword that the good Indexer will show his superiority over the commonplace worker. There are a large number of Indexes in which not only is the *best* heading *not* chosen but the very *worst* is. Thus in the Indexes to the *Canadian Journal*, a high-class magazine, we find such entries as the following, arranged under the word here printed in italics :—

A Monograph of the British Spongiadæ.
On the Iodide of Barium.
Sir Charles Barry, a Biography.
The late Professor Boole.
The Mohawk Language.

The same arrangement may be found in the Index to the Journal of the Society of Telegraph Engineers, thus—

A Strange Story.
Professor Wheatstone, original proposals, &c.

The handsome edition of Jewel's *Apology* by Isaacson (1825) contains an index which is worthy of special remark. It is divided into four alphabets, referring respectively to 1. Life ; 2. Apology ; 3. Notes to Life ; 4. Notes to Apology ; and this complicated machinery is attached to a book of only 286 pages. I think I may say that there is hardly an entry in the Index that would be of any use to the consulter, and to show that this censure is not too sweeping, I will add a few specimens :

Belief of a Resurrection.
Caution, Reformers proceeded with caution.
If Protestants are Heretics let the Papists prove them so from Scripture.
In withdrawing themselves from the Church of Rome, Protestants have not erred from Christ and his Apostles.
King John.
The Pope assumes Regal power and habit.
  Ditto employs spies.

In the " General Index to the Spectators, Tatlers and Guardians," referred to on a previous page, such words as Difference, Digression, Directions, Discourse, Dissertation and Instance, are specially noticed as bad headings in the original Indexes, which have been changed in the new one ; and yet these are the very words that are chosen by rule for headings in the British Museum Catalogue. Could any plan be adopted by which the following books would more thoroughly be hidden out of sight than by the present arrangement :

Kind. A Kind of a Dialogue in Hudibrasticks ; designed for the use of the Unthinking and Unlearned (1739).
Kinds. How to make several kinds of miniature pumps and a fire engine ; a book for boys (1860).

Some bibliographers always prefer substantives to adjectives as headings, but the whole point of a sentence is often contained in a substantival adjective. When adjective and substantive are joined to represent one idea, as Alimentary Canal, English History, they should be treated as compound nouns, and arranged under the letters *A* and *E* respectively.[1] The most marked example of an opposite rule that I have ever seen is to be found in the Index to Hare's *Walks in London* (1878). Here all the Alleys, Bridges, Buildings, Churches, Courts, Houses, Streets, etc., are arranged under those headings, and not under the proper name of each. There may be a certain advantage in some of these headings, but few would look for Lisson Grove under Grove, and the climax of absurdity is reached when Chalk Farm is placed under *Farm*. The adopted rule is not rigidly carried out, for Grey Friars will be found under G, and Austin Friars under F. Another peculiarity of this index is that a copy of it is added to each volume.

Books of facts are much easier indexed than books of opinion; but it. is most important that the contents of the latter should be properly registered. Some indexers seem to be of opinion that proper names are the most important items in an index, and while carefully including all these, they omit facts and opinions of much greater importance. As a rule it is objectionable when the consulter finds no additional information in the book to what is already given in the index; for instance, should the observation be made respecting a certain state of mind that " the Duke of Wellington probably felt the same at the Battle of Waterloo," it will be well for the indexer to pass the remark by unnoticed, as should he make the following entries, the consulter is not likely to be in a very genial mood when he looks up the references :

Waterloo, the Duke of Wellington's supposed feelings at the battle of.
Wellington (Duke of), his supposed feelings at Waterloo.

The hackneyed quotation of

Best, Mr. Justice, his great mind,

cannot be omitted here, although I am unable to give any satisfactory account of its origin. It forms an excellent example of the useless references to which we have just referred, and contains as well a ludicrous misapprehension of the passage

[1] See Rule 9, on page 72.

indexed, which is said to have been: "Mr. Justice Best said that he had a great mind to commit the man for trial." There can be no doubt that the entry, whether it ever occurred in an Index or not, was intended as a personal fling against Sir William Draper Best, puisne judge of the King's Bench from 1819 to 1824, and Lord Chief Justice of the Common Pleas from 1824 to 1829, in which latter year he resigned, and was created Lord Wynford. The story was told to Mr. Solly by Sir W. Domville, in 1825, and with reference to the index to one of Chitty's Law Books. Another friend tells me that he has a faint recollection that Chitty had a grudge against Best, and took an opportunity of expending his bile in this entry; but the late Dr. Doran insisted that the author of the joke was Leigh Hunt, who first published it in the *Examiner*. In this unsettled state we must leave the question, for it is not worth while to search the files of a newspaper in order to find the truth of so insignificant a matter.

The form in which the various entries in an index are to be drawn up is worthy of much attention, and particular care should be taken to expunge all redundant words. For instance, it will be better to write

> Smith (John), his character ; his execution.

than

> Smith (John), character of ; execution of.

or

> Brown (Robert) saves money.

than

> Brown (Robert), saving of money by.

Sometimes a characteristic adjective or adverb will help to give life and interest to the Index.

The indexer must aim at conciseness, but he should always specify the cause of reference, more especially in the case of proper names.[1] Few things are more annoying than to find a block list of references after a name, so that the consulter has to search through many pages before he can find what he seeks.[2] Mr. Markland draws particular attention to this point

---

[1] See Rule 10 on page 72.

[2] This evil is enlarged upon in a paper " On an ' Evitandum ' in Index-making, principally met with in French and German Periodical Scientific Literature, by B. R. Wheatley."—Transactions and Proceedings of the Conference of Librarians, 1877, pp. 88–92.

in a communication to the *Notes and Queries* (2nd series, vol. vii. p. 469) on the subject of Indexes. He complains bitterly of the Indexes to the collected edition of Walpole's Letters and to Scott's Swift. In the latter book there are 638 references to Harley, Earl of Oxford, without any indication of the reason why his name is entered in the Index. This case also affords a good instance of careless indexing in another particular, for these references are separated under different headings, instead of being gathered under one, as follows—

Harley (Robert)	227 references.	
Oxford (Lord)	111	,,
Treasurer, Lord Oxford	300	,,

Mr. Markland takes the opportunity of pointing out that good specimens of the right way to set out the references to an individual are to be found in Nichols's *Literary Anecdotes;* Hallam's *Constitutional History;* and Campbell's *Lives of the Lord Chancellors.* Probably the most colossal instance of the fault above alluded to is to be found in Ayscough's elaborate Index to the *Gentleman's Magazine,* where all the references under one surname are placed together without even the distinction of the Christian name. Mr. Solly made a curious calculation as to the time that would be employed in looking up these references. For instance, under the name *Smith,* there are 2411 entries, all " en masse," and with no initial letters. If there were these divisions, one would find " Zachary Smith " in a few minutes, but now one must look to each reference to find what is wanted. With taking down the volumes, and hunting through long lists of names, Mr. Solly found that each reference cost him two minutes of time, a by no means extravagant estimate; hence it would take the consulter eight days (working steadily ten hours a day) to find out if there be any note about Zachary Smith in the Magazine, a task so awful to think of that it may be presumed that no one will ever attempt it.

In some books a man will merely be referred to as holding an acre of land, or as having been seen by the author on a certain day. In these instances a specific cause of reference can hardly be given, but the difficulty may be got over by setting out the various entries in which some fact or opinion is mentioned, and then gathering together the remainder under the heading of *Alluded to*.

One would imagine that correctness of reference was the *sine qua non* of an index, and yet careless compilers, to save themselves trouble, have sometimes neglected this great essential. Books have been published with indexes that contained no reference at all, and until late years glossaries have usually been compiled without references to the places where the different words are used.

Mr. Peacock has drawn my attention to the reprint of Whitelock's *Memorials*, published by the University of Oxford in 1853. The original edition is in one volume folio (1682, reprinted 1732), and the new edition is in four volumes octavo, but, to save expense, the *old* index was printed to the *new* book. The difficulty was in part got over by giving the pages of the 1732 edition in the margin; but, as may be imagined, it is a most troublesome business to find anything by it. If the old index were a good one, there might be some excuse for its retention; but it is thoroughly bad, and all the mere misprints are retained in the new one. As a specimen of the extreme inaccuracy of the compilation, it may be mentioned that under one heading of 34 entries Mr. Peacock detected seven blunders, and, moreover, he does not think that this is at all an unfavourable specimen. Although Mr. Peacock has no statistics of the other entries, his experience leads him to believe that if any heading were taken at random, about one in four of the entries would be found to be misprinted.

An extreme case of misleading references is given in the Index of Authors appended to the old Classified Catalogue of the Library of Congress (Washington, 1840). The references here are not to pages but to chapters, and as some of the chapters extend over one hundred pages it may be guessed that a very tedious search has to be made; for instance, to find the reference *Abdy*, it is necessary to look over as many as seventy pages.

It has been said that a bad index is better than no index at all, but this is open to question, as the incomplete index deceives the consulter. We have fair warning of this incompleteness in *The Register of Corpus Christi Guild, York*, published by the Surtees Society in 1872, where we read on p. 321 — "This Index contains the names of all persons mentioned in the Appendix and foot-notes, but a selection only is given of those who were admitted into the Guild or enrolled in the Obituary." The plan here adopted is not to be commended, for it is clear that so important a name-list as this is should be thoroughly indexed. However learned and judicious an editor may be, we do not choose to submit to his judgment in the offhand decision of what is, and what is not—unimportant.

Many of the best indexes are indexes and something more; that is, information is added which may not be in the book itself, such as the date of birth and death of the persons mentioned, in order to distinguish between those bearing the same proper names. Mr. Ralph Thomas has added to his interesting notice of Quérard [1] (a pamphlet of 48 pages), an Index of eight pages. This index contains several such entries as the following :—

"Athenæum, The, no general index to, great literary want (and the Athenæum reproached the Edinburgh Review for remissness in not keeping up its indexes !).

The Index of Authors appended to De Morgan's Arithmetical Books, 1847, includes a list of reported Authors of works on Arithmetic which are not noticed in the book, but these of course have no mark of reference. By this means the Index shows the deficiencies of the book as well as its riches. It is needful, however, that the information added should be correct. An important example of the effect of wrong indexing is given in Merewether and Stephens's "History of Boroughs and Municipal Corporations." The word "Incorporation" is introduced into the index of the Patent Rolls without authority from the text, and long before there were incorporations in this country. The first actual use of the term is in the Charter of

---

[1] A Martyr to Bibliography: a Notice of the Life and Works of Joseph-Marie Quérard, Bibliographer . . . By Olphar Hamst, Esq. London (J. Russell Smith), 1867.

Incorporation of Hull (18. Henr. VI.), but upon the error in this index many other blunders have been founded.

The Indexer needs knowledge so as to be able to correct his author when necessary, for the most careful author will make slips occasionally, and it is highly satisfactory when the Indexer can set him right. He needs to be specially upon his guard in the case of misprints. Probably the most fruitful source of blundering is the confusion of the letters u and n. These are identical in old MSS., and consequently the copyist sometimes finds it difficult to decide which he shall use. In Capgrave's Chronicle of England is a reference to the "londe of Iude" [Judæa], but this is mis-spelt *Inde* in the edition published in the Master of the Rolls' series in 1858. Here we have a simple misprint which can easily be set right, but the Indexer has enlarged it into a wonderful blunder. Under the letter I is the following curious piece of information :—

"India . . . conquered by Judas Maccabeus and his brethren, 56." ! !

Many more instances of this confusion of the letters u and n might be given here, but two will suffice. George London was a very eminent horticulturist in his day, who, at the Revolution, was appointed Superintendent of the Royal Gardens, but he can seldom get his name properly spelt, because a later horticulturist has made the name Loudon more familiar. The reverse mistake was one made by the Duke of Wellington. C. J. Loudon (whose handwriting was not very legible) wrote to the Duke a request that he might see the Waterloo beeches at Stratfieldsaye. The letter puzzled the Duke, who knew nothing of the horticulturist, and read C. J. Loudon as C. J. London and beeches as breeches; so he wrote off to Bishop Blomfield that his Waterloo breeches disappeared long ago.

The worst blunders are not made by the ignorant, but by those who think themselves clever and jump to unwarranted conclusions; for instance, the compiler of a history of Norwich attributed a work on the Differential Calculus by a Fellow of St. John's College, Cambridge, to a medical practitioner of the town; but in order to make the subject more appropriate, he inserted the information in the following form—"to our respected fellow-townsman Mr. Arthur Brown we are indebted for a valuable treatise on *different calculi*"! There are few mistakes easier fallen into by Cataloguers and Indexers than that of rolling two men into one, and few blunders are less easily forgiven by the objects of the confusion; thus Bishop Jebb is said to have been in dismay when he found himself identified in Watt's *Bibliotheca Britannica* with his uncle the Unitarian writer. In Dircks's *Worcesteriana* (1866) there is a curious muddle of this kind. The first reprint of the Marquis of Worcester's *Century of Inventions* was issued by Thomas Payne, the highly respected bookseller of the Mews Gate, in 1746, but Mr. Dircks positively asserts that the "notorious Tom Paine" was the publisher of it, thus ignoring the different spelling of the two names.

A curious instance of uniting two men into one will be found in the *Athenæum* for May 13, 1871, where we read that "William Haidinger von Franz Ritter v. Hauer, the geologist and mineralogist, has died recently." What is here supposed to be one name is really the title of a biography of Haidinger by von Hauer.

There are a considerable number of names which have been created through the misreading of difficult words, and names of persons who never existed have by this means found their way into Biographical Dictionaries. In the Zoological Bibliography of Agassiz, there is an imaginary author, by name J. K. Broch, whose work, "Entomologische Briefe," was published in 1823. This pamphlet is anonymous, and written by one who signed himself J. K. *Broch.* is merely an explanation in the catalogue from which the entry was taken, that it was a brochure. Moreri created an author whom he styled "Dorus Basilicus" out of the title of James the First's *Δωρον βασιλικον*, and Bishop Walton supposed the title of the great Arabic Dictionary, the *Kamoos*, or Ocean, to be the name of an author whom he quotes as "Camus." In the *Biographie Universelle* there is a life of one "Nicholas Donis" by Baron Walckenaer, that name being a mere blundering alteration of "Dominus Nicholas," this Benedictine monk's true appellation. Thevenot, in his Travels, refers to the fables of "Damné et

Calilve," meaning the Hitopadesa or Pilpay's Fables. His translator calls them the fables of the damned Calilve. This is on a par with De Quincey's specimen of a French Abbe's Greek. Having to paraphrase the words "'Ηροδοτος και ιαζων," (Herodotus even while Ionicizing), the Frenchman rendered them "Herodote et aussi Jazon," thus creating a new author, one Jazon.[1] In the *Present State of Peru*, a compilation from the *Mercurio Peruano*, P. Geronymo Roman de la Higuera is transformed into "Father Geronymo, a Romance of La Higuera"! Well may we say to the worthy priest what Peter Quince said to Bottom, "Bless thee, bless thee, thou art translated."

The scissors-and-paste compilers are peculiarly liable to such errors as these, and Wilson Croker proved in the Quarterly Review that the *Memoires de Louis XVIII.* (published in 1832) was a mendacious compilation from the *Memoires de Bachaumont* by giving examples of the compiler's blundering. One of these muddles is well worth quoting, and it occurs in the following passage: "Seven bishops — of *Puy*, Gallard de Terraube; of *Langres*, La Luzerne; of *Rhodez*, Seignelay-Colbert; of *Gast*, Le Tria; of *Blois*, Laussiere Themines; of *Nancy*, Fontanges; of *Alais*, Beausset; of *Nevers*, Seguiran." Had the compiler taken the trouble to count his own list, he would have seen that he had given eight names instead of seven, and so have suspected that something was wrong; but he was not paid to think. The fact is that there is no such place as Gast, and was no such person as Le Tria. The Bishop of Rhodez was Seignelay-Colbert de Castle Hill, a descendant of the Scotch family of Cuthbert of Castle Hill, in Inverness-shire, and Bachaumont misled his successor by writing Gast Le Hill for Castle Hill. The introduction of a stop and a little misspelling originated the blunder as we now find it.

An author is sometimes turned into a place, as in the article on *Stenography* in Rees's Cyclopædia. John Nicolai published a Treatise on the Signs of the Ancients at the beginning of the last century, and the writer of the article having seen it stated that a certain fact was to be found in Nicolai, jumped to the conclusion that it was the name of a place and wrote: "It was

---

[1] De Quincey's Works, ed. 1862, vol. 8, p. 180.

at Nicolai that this method of writing was first introduced to the Greeks by Xenophon himself."

D'Israeli gives a few curious instances of supposed authors in his *Curiosities of Literature*—" A book was written in praise of Ciampini by Ferdinand Fabiani, who quoting a French narrative of travels in Italy, took for the name of the author the following words, found at the end of the title-page, *Enrichi de deux Listes*; that is, 'Enriched with two Lists:' on this he observes 'that Mr. Enriched with two Lists has not failed to do that justice to Ciampini which he merited.' The abridgers of Gesner's Bibliotheca ascribe the romance of *Amadis* to one *Acuerdo Olvido*: Remembrance, Oblivion. Not knowing that these two words on the title-page of the French version of that book formed the translator's Spanish motto. D'Aquin, the French King's physician, in his memoir on the preparation of Bark, takes *Mantissa*, which is the title of the Appendix to the History of Plants by Johnstone, for the name of an author, and who he says is so extremely rare, that he only knows him by name." To these may be added *S. Viar*, whose existence was supposed to be proved by an inscription until an antiquary showed that the complete reading of the mutilated stone was

PRÆFECTUS . VIARUM.

Also the *August Oriuna*, supposed to be the wife of Carausius, of whom Dr. Stukeley wrote some theoretical memoirs. This blunder originated in the credulous Doctor's misreading of the inscription on a battered coin of Carausius :—

ORIVNA AVG . *for* FORTVNA AVG.

The French often fall into this class of blunders from their constant practice of translating or explaining whatever it is supposed can be translated or explained, thus G. Brunet of Bordeaux, having occasion in his " La France Litteraire au xvᵉ Siecle," to mention " White Knights," the seat of the Duke of Marlborough, translates it " Le Chevalier Blanc." [1] When Dr. Buckland, the distinguished geologist, died, a certain French paper published a biography of him, in which it was explained that the deceased had been a very versatile writer, for

---

[1] Notice of Quérard, by Olphar Hamst. 1867.

besides his works on Geology, he had produced one, "Sur les ponts et chaussees." This was a puzzle at first, but it was soon found that the Bridgewater Treatise was here alluded to. The French love of translation and explanation is amusingly illustrated in the *Annuaire des Societes Savantes, par le Cte. Achmet d'Hericourt*, 1863, where the author, in his notice of the Geological and Polytechnic Society of the West Riding of Yorkshire, says that as it is known that the English word *Ride* means a "voyage a cheval ou en voiture," it might be thought that this was a "Societe hippique," but he obligingly adds that it is not so.

We have already seen in several cases how dangerous it is to jump to conclusions, but we have still to point out the particular danger of filling out contractions without sufficient knowledge. Pope, in a note on *Measure for Measure*, informs us that the story was taken from Giraldi Cinthio's novel Dec. 8, Nov. 5, thus contracting the words Decade and Novel. Warburton, in his edition of Shakespeare, was misled by these contractions, and filled them out as December 8, and November 5. An error of the same kind is made by Dr. Allibone in his Dictionary of English Literature, under the heading of Isaac Disraeli. He notices new editions of that author's works revised by the Right Hon. the Chancellor of the Exchequer, of course Isaac's son Benjamin (now Earl of Beaconsfield and Prime Minister); but unfortunately there were two Chancellors in 1858, and Allibone chooses the wrong one, printing as information to the reader that the reviser was Sir George Cornewall Lewis. But still worse was the following emendation of an 'intelligent' printer. A writer in one of the reviews sent his copy to press with the contraction "J. C. first invaded Britain," and the compositor, who made it his business to fill up all such abbreviations, instead of Julius Cæsar, set up *Jesus Christ*.[1]

Next in importance to the selection of appropriate headings

---

[1] A friend asks me to give chapter and verse for this blunder, but it will be seen that nothing is more difficult than to find an authority for misprints which are corrected as soon as they are found out, perhaps even in the proof. A curious misprint occurred in *The Times* in a letter from Lord Shaftesbury (August, 1878), who wrote of the Bulgarians that "they panted for liberty," but was made by the printer to say "they prated of liberty."

in an Index is the careful use of cross references. Great judgment is here required, as the consulters are naturally irritated by being referred backwards and forwards, particularly in a large Index. At the same time, if judiciously inserted, such references are a great help. When the entries are short and few, it is better to repeat them than to refer from one to the other. In the case of long entries cross references are very advantageous, and it is always well to refer to cognate headings.[1] This, however, must not be carried too far; for, as Mr. Poole says in an article on his own index,[2] "If every subject shall have cross references to its allies, the work will be mainly a book of cross references rather than an index of subjects." He adds, "One correspondent gives fifty-eight cross references under Mental Philosophy, and fifty-eight more might be added just as appropriate."

At all events let the cross references be real. In Eadie's Dictionary of the Bible (1850), there is a reference "Dorcas *see* Tabitha," but there is no entry under Tabitha at all.

No reference to the contents of a general heading which is without subdivision should be allowed.[3] There are too many of these vague cross references in the Penny Cyclopædia, where you are referred from the known to the unknown. If a general heading be divided into sections, and each of these be clearly defined, they should be cross referenced, but not otherwise. At present you may look for Pesth and be referred to Hungary, where probably there is much about Pesth, but you do not know where to look for it in the long article without clue. Sometimes cross references are mere expedients, particularly in the case of a cyclopædia published in volumes or numbers. Thus a writer agrees to contribute an article early in the alphabet, but is not ready

[1] See Rule 11, p. 72.
[2] Library Journal.
[3] My brother (Mr. B. R. Wheatley) writes as follows of Allibone's forty Indexes: "What however shall we say of the sub-indexes which really have no existence whatever, except in the list of their titles at the commencement? Take, for instance, the first—Alchemy—which refers you to Class or Index 8, which is Chemistry. How much nearer are you to Alchemy?—it is a more secret science in the Index than it was in the middle ages—you have 500 names under Chemistry, and you must look out the whole of them before you find the philosopher's stone which lies hid in this five-century crucible of mixed ingredients."—Trans. Conference of Librarians, 1877.

in time for the publication of the part, so a cross reference is inserted which sends the reader to a synonym later on in the alphabet. In certain cases this has been done two or three times. In Cobbett's *Woodlands* there is a good specimen of backwards and forwards cross referencing. The author writes: "Many years ago I wished to know whether I could raise birch trees from the *seed*. . . . . I then looked into the great book of knowledge, the Encyclopædia Britannica; there I found in the general dictionary—

> BIRCH TREE.—See *Betula* (Botany Index).

I hastened to BETULA with great eagerness and there I found—

> BETULA.—See *Birch* Tree.

That was all, and this was pretty encouragement."

Cross referencing has its curiosities as well as other branches of our subject. Perhaps the most odd collection of cross references are to be found in Hawkins's *Pleas of the Crown,* of which it was said in the *Monthly Magazine* for June, 1801 (p. 419) "A plain unlettered man is led to suspect that the writer of the volume and the writer of the index are playing at cross purposes." The following are some of the most amusing entries, but there are many more as good:

Assault, *see* Son.	Farthing, *see* Halfpenny.
Cards, *see* Dice.	Fear, *see* Robbery.
Cattle, *see* Clergy.	Footway, *see* Nuisance.
Chastity, *see* Homicide.	Honour, *see* Constable.
Coin, *see* High Treason.	King, *see* Treason.
Convicts, *see* Clergy.	London, *see* Outlawry.
Death, *see* Appeal.	Shop, *see* Burglary.
Election, *see* Bribery.	Sickness, *see* Bail.

The Index to Ford's Handbook of Spain contains an amusing reference—

> Wellington, *see* Duke.

But perhaps the strangest place to find a cross reference is on a tombstone. In Barnes churchyard the following inscription was put up to a once famous actor:—

> Mr. J. Moody
> A native of the Parish of Saint Clement Danes
> and an old Member of Drury Lane Theatre.
> For his Memoirs see the European Magazine ; for his professional
> abilities see Churchill's Rosciad.
> Obiit Dec. 26 1812,
> Anno Ætatis 85.

II.

Intimately connected with compilation is arrangement, for however well the contents of a book may be analysed, the result will not form a good Index unless it is well arranged.

An Index should be one and indivisible, and not broken up into several alphabets, thus every work ought to have its complete Index whether it is one volume or many.[1] This important rule has frequently been neglected in English books, and is almost universally rejected in Foreign ones, to the great inconvenience of readers. An Index may be arranged either chronologically, alphabetically, or according to classes, but great confusion will be caused by uniting the three. The alphabetical arrangement is so simple, so convenient, and so easily understood by all, that it has naturally superseded the other forms, but some still cling to the rags of classification, in the belief that that is a more scientific arrangement. The evil of this is that the consulter is never sure whether the reference he requires may not be lurking in some place that he has missed, but in the case of a single alphabet an answer to the question "Does the Index contain what I require?" is obtained at once. Classification is the reverse of this, for, as Mr. Poole says in his observations on the proposal of one of his helpers to place Wealth, Finance, and Population under the head of Political Economy—"the fatal defect of every classified arrangement is that nobody understands it except the person who made it and he is often in doubt." The general principle here enunciated will perhaps be better understood by reference to a few examples. Brayley's *Surrey*, in five volumes, has a separate Index to each volume, and it is a pretty general experience that whatever is wanted is sure to be found in the last volume consulted. The new edition of Hutchins's *Dorset*, 1874, has at the end eight separate Indexes, 1. Places; 2. Pedigrees; 3. Persons; 4. Arms; 5. Blazons; 6. Glossarial; 7. Domesday; 8. Inquisitions. How much thought is here required which would not be needed were all united into one alphabet. The general Index to the Reports of

---

[1] See Rules 1 and 2, p. 71.

the British Association is a most inconvenient one to use, as it is split up into six alphabets; but the evil of these subdivisions is most marked in Indexes to the various volumes of the *Athenæum*, which are so subdivided that they are practically useless. Who would rack his brain to find under which of the many headings the subject he requires is likely to be hidden? These divided Indexes are the exception in English books, but abroad almost every Index is in two parts: 1. Persons; 2. Things. The Index to Arago's complete works has the threefold division: 1. Auteurs; 2. Cosmique; 3. Matieres. If this division be made, it ought surely to be carried out correctly, and yet in the *Autoren Register* to Carus' and Engelmann's Bibliography of Zoology may be found the following entries: *Schreiben; Schriften; Zu* Humboldts Cosmos; *Zur* Fauna.

The inconveniences of classification in an index are so palpable that it is needless to add more, but a list of titles of books that have given trouble to bibliographers, and at sundry times have been misarranged, will perhaps be amusing. Edgeworth's Essay on Irish Bulls and a Treatise on the Great Seal have been placed under the heading of *Zoology;* Napier's Bones under *Anatomy;* Swinburne's Under the Microscope under *Optical Instruments;* a volume of Poems, entitled the Viol and Lute, under *Musical Instruments;* Ruskin's Notes on the Construction of Sheepfolds under *Agriculture;* McEwen on the Types under *Printing;* and most famous of all, Link, de Stellis Marinis, under *Astronomy.* Disraeli reports an amusing anecdote of "an honest friar who compiled a church history and placed in the class of ecclesiastical writers Guarini, the Italian poet; this arose from a most risible blunder: on the faith of the title of his celebrated amorous pastoral *Il Pastor Fido,* 'The Faithful Shepherd,' our good father imagined that the character of a curate, vicar, or bishop, was represented in this work."

Such incongruities as these had a charm for the author of the *Curiosities of Literature,* and he therefore devotes a chapter to the "Titles of Books." The foregoing are tempting subjects for the jumpers to conclusions, but some titles are impenetrable —what, for instance, can be made of *Labia Dormientum?* It turns out to be a Catalogue of rabbinical writers, and was so called in reference to a passage in *Solomon's Song,* " Like the best wine for my beloved, that goeth down sweetly, causing *the lips of those that are asleep to speak* " (vii. 19).

In order to help the makers of Indexes in judging of the relative extent of the various letters of the Alphabet certain calculations have been made,[1] but the statistics must vary greatly according to the character of the Index. Thus B is the largest in an Index of English names, but loses its pre-eminence in an Index of subjects, and *S* takes high rank in both classes.

Mr. Curtis advocates in his paper the arrangement under each initial letter according to the next following vowel, a plan often adopted in Locke's and other Common Place Books, but which is highly inconvenient, especially when words without a second vowel as *Ash* and *Epps* are placed at the head of each letter, as *Ash* before *Adam* and *Abel;* and *Epps* before *Ebenezer.*

In arranging entries in alphabetical order it is necessary to sort them up to the most minute difference of spelling. In order to save themselves trouble some workers think they may leave off sorting at the third letter, and their idleness gives others much annoyance. I have often been troubled in this way when consulting the Index to a large map of England in which the names of places are not arranged further than the third letter.

The Alphabetical arrangement has its difficulties which must be overcome ; for instance, it looks awkward when the plural comes before the singular, and the adjective before the substantive from which it is formed, as *naval* and *navies* before *navy.*

Another difficulty arises when names and words from a foreign language are introduced into an English Index. The only safe rule in these cases is to use the English alphabet.[2] One of the Rules of the American Library Association is, " The German *ae, oe, ue* are always to be written a, o, u, and arranged

---

[1] " On the best method of constructing an Index, by F. A. Curtis, of the Eagle Insurance Office," in the *Assurance Magazine,* vol. 8 (1858), pp. 54–57. See also *Notes and Queries,* 2nd S. vi. 496, 3rd S. iv. 371.

[2] See Rule 3.

as a, o, u "; by this Goethe would have to be written Gothe, which is now an unusual form, and I think it would be better to insist that where both forms are used, one or other should be chosen and all instances spelt alike. It is a very common practice to arrange a, o, u, as if they were written ae, oe, ue, but this leads to the greatest confusion, and no notice should be taken of letters that are merely to be understood. Those who have stumbled over the arrangement that treats the vowel I and consonant J, and the vowel U and consonant V, as identical, will be glad to have a rule that keeps them distinct.

Although it has been previously said that words and names must be arranged in alphabet up to their last letters, it is necessary to bear in mind that each word is to stand by itself; for instance, first will come the various persons bearing the surname *Grave*, arranged according to the order of their Christian names,

> Grave, George,
> Grave, John,

then the substantive and adjective *grave*, arranged according to the alphabet of the words that follow,

> Grave at Kherson,
> Grave of Hope,
> Grave Thoughts,

and last,

> Gravelot,
> Gravesend.[1]

We now come to the consideration of a matter of some perplexity. It is more of a difficulty for the Cataloguer than for the Indexer, still it is one with which the latter must grapple. There cannot be two opinions about the simple rule that a man should be set down under his surname, but our trouble commences when we ask the question—What is a surname? The answer to it must necessarily be complicated on account of the varieties of form which proper names take in different languages. The greatest difficulty arises from the prefixes, some of which can easily be dispensed with, while others are integral portions of the name.[2] If the prefix be a preposition, it must be rejected, and the name arranged in alphabet under the

---

[1] Rule 4. [2] See Rule 5.

following letter ; thus, *D'*, *De*, in French, *Da* in Italian,[1] *Von*
in German, and *Van* in Dutch, are no real portion of foreign
names, which can stand very well without them. If, however,
the prefix be an article, such as the French *La*, it must be
retained ; for instance, the full name of the great astronomer
La Place is De La Place, but it is under L that it could alone
be placed with propriety. If no other reason could be given,
a very sufficient one might be found in the fact that were
not *De* and *Von* rejected, a large proportion of French and
German names would appear respectively under those prefixes.
Although this rule is generally accepted as the only true one, it
is seldom carried out consistently ; thus in the South Kensington
Universal Catalogue of Books on Art, we find D'Ayzac under
Ayzac, D'Azara under *D*, D'Azeglio under *A*, De La Blanchere
under *D*, De La Borde under *L*, De La Fons under both *D* and
L, with a cross reference from Fons. A logical difficulty arises
when the preposition is joined to the article, as in *Du* and *Des*,
and here, in order to retain the article, we are forced to retain
the preposition as well. These rules only apply to Foreign
names, and such English names as De Quincey, Delabeche,
Van Mildert, must be arranged under *D* and *V* respectively,
because the prefixes are here meaningless.

The rule for the arrangement of compound names differs
accordingly as these names are either English or Foreign.[2] The
frequent practice in England of using surnames as baptismal
names gives the united names the appearance of compound
names, which they really are not. The first name in a foreign
compound is almost invariably the true name, and frequently
the second name is that of the owner's wife or mother. The
French cannot understand our sur-christian-names, and with few
exceptions treat them as true surnames. There is a most amusing
blunder consequent on this misapprehension in the well-known
Biographie Moderne, edited by the late Dr. Hoefer, and published by Firmin Didot. In this valuable Biographical
Dictionary there is a long account of Brigham Young, extend-
ing over many columns, but, instead of appearing under Y,
it has a place found for it in letter B, and the heading runs as

[1] *Da* in Portuguese is a compound of preposition and article.
[2] See Rule 8.

follows: "Brigham le jeune ou Brigham Young"! Although such an instance as this could not well be paralleled in any English book of the same high character, we are not as a nation incapable of making blunders of a like kind. De Morgan remarks, in his Arithmetical Books, "I have had in one or two instances to throw away German *Authors* for a very obvious reason. The reader will not find the works of *Anleitung* or *Grundriss* or *Rechenbuch* in my list, which is more than can be said of every one that has preceded it." *Derselbe* might have been added, as it sometimes has a very surname-like look. Blunders are of no particular nationality, and it is needful to use special vigilance in transferring proper names from the books of one language to those of another. The most trustful, however, would be on his guard when dealing with a writer who introduced the Duke of Newcastle to his readers as "Gul. de Cavendy dux de Xeucathle."

Sometimes we have to deal with the latinised names of celebrated men, and it is a very frequent practice to turn these back into the vernacular, but it may be questioned whether it is right to do so. De Morgan writes, "I have not attempted to translate the names of those who wrote in Latin at a time when that language was the universal medium of communication. . . . . It is well to know that Copernicus, Dasypodius, Xylander, Regiomontanus, and Clavius were Zepernik, Rauchfuss, Holtzmann, Muller and Schlussel. But as the butcher's bills of these eminent men are lost, and their writings only remain, it is best to designate them by the name which they bear on the latter rather than on the former."

The question however has pertinently been asked, how are we to act if the butchers' bills were by chance to be forthcoming and required registration in a Catalogue of Manuscripts. Probably in this case also it would be well to arrange the names under their best known forms. The Hungarians, and sometimes the Italians, place the surname before the Christian name, which is very confusing to those unacquainted with the practice. Sometimes the same difficulty occurs in English from the manner in which the names are printed; thus we learn from the *Gentleman's Magazine* that

Owen Gallager
Fleetwood Hesketh } died in 1769.

The Index-maker indexed these as *Gallager* and *Fleetwood!*
so that the death of Mr. Gallager may easily be found, but the
date of Mr. Hesketh's death cannot be found at all. The
change of family name is a source of confusion to those unacquainted with the niceties of genealogy. Mr. Solly draws my
attention to a case of this kind in which the Heskeths changed
their name in 1806 to Bamford by Act of Parliament, and then
subsequently obtained another Act to change it back to Hesketh.
Now the name is Lloyd-Hesketh-Bamford-Hesketh, which is
almost as complicated a series as Edward George Earle Lytton
Bulwer Lytton, Lord Lytton.[1] This leads us to the rule by
which peers are to be arranged under their titles instead of their
family names.[2] The most usual and certainly most natural
practice is so to arrange them, but the British Museum rule is
the reverse, and Mr. Cutter followed the Museum rule in his
full rules, although he did not approve of it. In the short
rules drawn up by Mr. Cutter and a Committee of the American
Library Association[3] this is judiciously altered and some sound
reasons are given for the later decision. The definition of a
name as "that by which a person or thing is known" would
naturally lead to the choice of Chesterfield as the name of the
author of Chesterfield's Letters, because Stanhope is the name
by which he is not known. It is further added—

"In regard to one objection urged against entry under the title, that it
brings together members of different families who at various times have
had the same title, and that it separates members of the same family who
have held different titles, the Committee cannot see what this has to do
with the question. The works of the various Smiths are put side by side
in the Catalogue, not because their authors belong to the same family,
which may or may not be the case, but because their names are spelled
alike and must be put together if they are ever to be found in a Catalogue
which is arranged alphabetically. If the son of James Smith chooses to
uniformly spell his name Smythe he will be put not with the ancestral
Smiths, but among the Smy's, because he will be looked for there ; and
if he is Duke of Abercorn he should be put under Abercorn for the same

---

[1] " When I asked his name, said, in a thick, gobbling kind of voice :
 ' Sawedwadgeorgeearllittnbulwig.'
 ' Sir what ?' says I quite agast at the same.
 ' Sawedwad—no, I mean Mistawedwad Lyttn Bulwig.' "
 —Thackeray's *Memoirs of Mr. Charles J. Yellowplush.*

[2] See Rule 7.
[3] Library Journal, vol. iii. No. 1.

reason. A Catalogue is not a biographical dictionary or a genealogical table, and its efficiency is in danger of being lessened if its makers confound the two purposes." [1]

In some instances, such as Horace Walpole, the name by which the great letter writer is always known, the rule must be broken, but double references should be adopted in all doubtful cases; thus Bulwer's novels cannot be ignored, although their author's name must be treated as Lytton. Apropos of the sound rule that all theories as to the separation of different members of the same family must be disregarded, we may mention the case of a great composer. It would be impossible to arrange the name of Meyerbeer under any other letter than *M*, although by doing so we place him under his Christian name, and separate him from his scientific brother Beer. There can hardly be a greater absurdity than to ferret out a man's earliest name, and place him under that. In the British Museum Catalogue the works of Sir Francis Palgrave are entered under *Cohen*, a name which 999 persons out of every thousand never heard of in connexion with him.

Bishops, deans and others, holding official titles, must always be arranged under their family names. It has been objected that reasons which apply to peers apply also to them; but this is not really the case, for a bishop is frequently referred to by his surname during his lifetime, and always so after his death. He has but a life interest in the name of his see. To illustrate this I would mention two eminent contemporaries—John Churchill, Duke of Marlborough, and Gilbert Burnet, Bishop of Salisbury. We know the one as Duke of Marlborough and the other as Bishop Burnet, and we should naturally turn to M. and B. respectively for their names.

There are a few minor matters worthy of mention in this department of name headings. The initials which stand for Christian names often give much trouble, particularly among foreigners. Most Frenchmen consider themselves too important and well known to need the use of Christian names, and therefore *M.* usually stands for *Monsieur;* this cannot, however, be taken for granted without inquiry, for it sometimes

---

[1] American Library Association Report (Library Journal, vol. iii. No. 1, March, 1878, p. 15, col. 1).

means *Michel* or other Christian name commencing with *M*. I have noticed in a German periodical[1] some extreme cases of the careless use of initials; and the three following will afford good specimens of this: 1. H. D. Gerling; 2. H. W. Brandes; 3. D. W. Olbers. Here all three cases look alike, but in the first H. D. represent two titles—Herr Doctor; in the second H. W. represent two Christian names—Heinrich Wilhelm; and in the third, one title and one Christian name are intended —Dr. W. Olbers. To some these points will appear trivial, but they are not so to those who have undergone endless trouble in unravelling the enigmas. The indexer should insert the names of persons in all simplicity, and ruthlessly omit the Mr. so frequently used by his author.[2] It was the neglect of this rule which angered Dr. Johnson. Boswell records how, happening to mention Mr. Flaxman, a dissenting minister, with some compliment to his exact memory in chronological matters, the Dr. replied, 'Let me hear no more of him, Sir. That is the fellow who made the Index to my Ramblers, and set down the name of Milton thus: Milton, *Mr.* John.' "

It is amusing to find that in spite of this ebullition no means were taken to remedy the evil. Johnson died in 1784, and yet in the twelfth edition of the *Rambler*, dated 1791, which is now before me, I find the same dishonouring title still retained. Besides *Mr.* Milton, notices of *Mr.* Richard Baxter, *Mr.* Abraham Cowley, *Mr.* John Dryden, *Mr.* Alexander Pope, and *Mr.* Edmund Spenser will be found in the Index.

Oddities in names give trouble, and are frequently the cause of blunders; for instance, there are living at the same time grandfather, father and grandson, who all bear the same names. To distinguish himself, the grandson adds the word *Tertius* to his name, and his card is printed as *John Smith Ter.* Now 'Ter' is so unusual an affix that a hurried cataloguer or indexer might almost be excused for treating it as Mr. Smith's surname.

The signatures of Peers and Bishops are a source of trouble

[1] Lindenau, Zeitschrift für Astronomie, 1816.
[2] In the case of little known men, whose Christian names are not given, it may sometimes be necessary to use the Mr.; for instance, in Pepys's Diary, if this word were not added to certain of the persons mentioned, there would often be confusion between the names of persons and of places.

to many, thus a certain eminent bookseller is said to have once
received a letter signed 'George Winton,' proposing the publication of a life of Pitt, but, as he did not know the name, he
paid no attention to the letter, and was much astonished when
he afterwards learnt that his correspondent was no less a person
than Pitt's friend and former tutor, George Pretyman Tomline
Bishop of Winchester. This is akin to the mistake of the
Scotch doctor attending on the Princess Charlotte during her
illness, who said that 'ane Jean Saroom' had been continually
making inquiries, but not knowing the fellow he had taken no
notice of him. Thus the Bishop of Salisbury was treated with
contempt by one totally ignorant of his dignity. There is a
reverse case of a catalogue made by a worthy bookseller of the
name of *William London,* which was long supposed to be the
work of Dr. William Juxon, the Bishop of London at the time
of publication.

A very amusing blunder of this class is said to have occurred
lately. A certain person received a document signed "Richmond & Gordon," and being imperfectly acquainted with the
refinements of the peerage, he directed his answer for the
Duke to "Messrs. Richmond and Gordon."

It has been suggested that all lists of errata in books should
be indexed, and there is no doubt that the chief items in these
lists should be referred to, as they are otherwise likely to be
overlooked. It is worse than useless to refer to a mis-statement
in the text without reference to the place where it is set right.
This hint is the more important, in that these mistakes are
frequently repeated without any notice being taken of the
overlooked *errata.* The errata pointed out in Sir Thomas
Browne's *Religio Medici* (1643) were not corrected in subsequent
editions, and many other books have remained in similar case.
The first book with a printed errata is the Venice Juvenal of
1478, previously the mistakes had been corrected by the pen.
One of the longest lists of errata on record is in the edition of
the works of Picus of Mirandula, printed by Knoblauch of
Strasburg in 1507, which occupies fifteen folio pages. An
English printer, however, has managed to distance the foreigner
in the race of carelessness, for a little book of only 172 pages,
entitled the "Anatomy of the Mass," 1561, has also a list of

errata of fifteen pages. Dr. Johnson, referring in his *Life of Lord Lyttelton* to his subject's *History of Henry II.* (1773), speaks of the 19 pages of errata as something which "the world had hardly seen before." Disraeli gives, in his *Curiosities of Literature*, some amusing instances of misreadings purposely inserted in the text, with the sole object of being corrected in the errata. Wherever the Inquisition had any power, particularly at Rome, the use of the word fatum or fata in any book was strictly prohibited. An author desirous of using the latter word, adroitly invented this scheme : he had printed in his book *facta*, and in the errata he put, for *facta* read *fata*. Scarron did the same thing on another occasion. He had composed some verses, at the head of which he placed this dedication : *A Guillemette, chienne de ma Sœur ;* but, having a quarrel with his sister, he maliciously put in the *errata*, instead of *Chienne de ma Sœur* read *ma chienne de Sœur*.

III.

Some Indexers suppose that their work is complete when they have made their Index, but they need to prepare their copy for the press, and also to see that their instructions are carried out by the printer. Much of the value of an Index depends upon the mode in which it is printed, and every endeavour should be made to set it out with clearness. It was not the practice in old Indexes to bring the Indexed word to the front, but to leave it in its place in the sentence, so that the alphabetical order was not made perceptible to the eye. This is now changed, but the evil still exists in the newspaper lists of Births, Deaths and Marriages, more especially in those of the *Times*. When the penny papers were started they introduced the improvement of setting the name at the beginning of the entry as a heading. The *Times* took the hint from its less august contemporaries, but would not condescend to copy them completely, so that the extent of the change was the printing of the names in small capitals. It is to be hoped that at some future day this pride may be overcome and the public be allowed to enjoy the convenience

of reading the name first. The inconvenience of the present
system is greatest in the marriage advertisements, where the
officiating clergy, about whom the reader cares nothing, take
precedence, and crowd out of sight the hero and heroine. *Punch*
had a good skit on this nuisance once, and said that when a
poor man was thus hidden under a pile of parsons it became
impossible to know what really had happened to him ; whether
he was in fact born, married, dead, or bankrupt !

Where the reduction of space is not an object, the titles of
each article should be made to occupy a separate line, by which
means the headings are brought more prominently before the
eye. There are few points in which the printer is more likely
to go wrong (if not watched) than in the use of marks of repetition, and many otherwise good Indexes are full of the
most perplexing instances of their misapplication. The dash
is a far better mark of repetition than mere indentation, but
it must be kept for entries exactly similar.[1] The neglect of
this rule leads to the perpetration of the greatest absurdities,
thus the oft-quoted instance—

> " Mill on Liberty
> —— on the Floss."

is not an invention, but actually occurred in a catalogue. The
following are good examples of what to avoid.

From the Index of the *Companion to the Almanac* (Lond. 1843)

> New Albion
> —— Annuities
> —— Bread
> —— Brentford
> Bartholomew Massacre
> ————— Lane
> Brimstone, duty on
> ————— butterfly
> Cotton, Sir Willoughby
> ——, price of,
> Old Stratford Bridge
> —– Style
> —– Swinford

---

[1] See Rule 17.

From the Index of *Pepys's Diary* (various editions)

Child, Mr.
—— of Hales, the, a giant
Court ladies, masculine attire of the
—— of Arches
Fish, method of preserving
——, Mrs.
Ireland, state of affairs in, &c.
——, a cooper
Katherine Hall, Cambridge
———— Pear
———— of Valois
———— the Man of War
———— Yacht
Kentish Knock, the, a Shoal
—— Town
Lamb's Conduit
—— Wool
Old age
—— Artillery Yard
—— Bailey
Orange Moll
——, old Prince of
Scotland, state of
———— Yard

The opposite evil of repeating the heading, even when identical, is rarer, but almost as confusing.

It is so easy to confuse two men of the same name together that every help towards keeping them distinct which the printer can give should be adopted. We have already drawn attention to this point, but it is so important a matter that the reader will perhaps excuse the insertion here of two more anecdotes to close the subject with. An Englishman on a visit to the United States carried with him a letter of introduction to Dr. Channing, but through inadvertence he called upon the great man's brother, who was a physician. The doctor soon found out that the visit was not intended for him, so he said to the Englishman : " You have made a mistake, it is the Dr. Channing who preaches that you want, I am the Dr. Channing who practises."

Very sore feelings are apt to be engendered between men who

are constantly being confused together, and in the following case one of the parties did not adopt the means best suited to heal differences, but laid himself open to a well-merited rebuke. Two men bearing the same names lived in the same country town. One was a clergyman of the Church of England, and the other was a Dissenting minister. On a certain occasion the clergyman received a letter intended for the minister, which he forwarded with a note to this effect—"Had you not taken a title (Rev.) to which you have no claim, this mistake would not have occurred." Shortly afterwards a parcel containing some lithographed sermons intended for the clergyman were delivered by mistake to the minister, who sent them on with this note—"Had you not undertaken an office for which you appear to be unfitted, this mistake would not have occurred."

In the previous pages a few of the chief difficulties of the Index-maker have been commented upon : stumbling-blocks with which he is too well acquainted, but which are very generally ignored by others. He must endeavour to attain perfection, but he will always have the unpleasant feeling that something may have been missed, and so strong was this feeling with a contributor to the *Notes and Queries* that he sent the following acrostic as a motto for an Index :—[1]

> I   I
> N   never
> D   did
> E   ensure
> X   exactness

The Index maker of modern days must needs depend upon himself, for he has not the help that the young man mentioned by Giraldus had when he could discern the false passages in a book by the crowd of devils which they attracted. Such *devils* as these would be invaluable in a printing office !

If, however, the Indexer, in common with the Bibliographer, has his troubles, he has his reward, for we have already seen that the claims of a big book to notice have been grounded upon its possession of a good index, and De Morgan, when entering his own Elements of Arithmetic in the account of

---

[1] 2nd Series, vol. i. p. 481.

Arithmetical Books, writes :—" Books of Bibliography last longer than elementary works, so that I have a chance of standing in a list to be made two centuries hence, which the book itself would certainly not procure me."

There is, therefore, hope for us that when our other works are forgotten, we may still live as the compilers of an index.

[Since the previous pages have been printed off, I have been told by Dr. Greenhill of Hastings that our late learned friend Thomas Watts of the British Museum spoke to him about the formation of an Index Society as early as the year 1842.

I am also able, through the kindness of Mr. Macray, to illustrate the printer's blunder on page 53 from a work by one of the most careful and trustworthy of editors, viz., " Historie of . . . Edward IV. 1471," edited by John Bruce 1838 (Camden Society). At p. 7 we read : " Wherefore the Kynge may say as Julius Cæsar sayde, he that is nat agaynst me is with me."]

The following rules have been drawn up by the Committee, in order to obtain uniformity in the compilation of their Indexes. They are not considered as final, and can be added to as occasion may require.

In some few points the respective rules for Cataloguing and for Indexing are identical, but in the majority of instances the rules made for the former will not apply to the latter.

Those who require rules for Cataloguing should obtain the British Museum Rules, Mr. Cutter's full Rules, forming the second part of the Special Report on American Libraries, and the short Rules drawn up by a Committee of the American Library Association, and printed in the Library Journal.

RULES FOR OBTAINING UNIFORMITY IN THE INDEXES OF BOOKS.

1.—Every work should have one Index for the whole set and not an Index to each volume.

2.—Indexes to be arranged in Alphabetical Order:—proper names and subjects being united in *one* alphabet. An Introduction, containing some indication of the classification of the contents of the book indexed, to be prefixed.

3.—The entries to be arranged according to the order of the English Alphabet. I and J, and U and V, to be kept distinct.

4.—Headings consisting of two or more distinct words are not to be treated as integral portions of one word, thus the arrangement should be:—

Grave, John,		Grave at Kherson.
Grave at Kherson		Grave, John.
Grave of Hope	not	Gravelot.
Grave Thoughts		Grave of Hope.
Gravelot		Gravesend.
Gravesend		Grave Thoughts.

5.—Proper Names of foreigners to be alphabetically arranged under the prefixes:—

Dal		*Dal Sie.*
Del		*Del Rio.*
Della		*Della Casa.*
Des	as	*Des Cloiseaux.*
Du		*Du Bois.*
La		*La Condamine.*
Le		*Le Sage.*

but *not* under the prefixes:—

D'	as	*Abbadie*	not	*D'Abbadie.*
Da	,,	*Silva*	,,	*Da Silva.*
De	,,	*La Place*	,,	*De La Place.*
Von	,,	*Humboldt*	,,	*Von Humboldt.*
Van	,,	*Beneden*	,,	*Van Beneden.*

It is an acknowledged principle that when the prefix is a preposition it is to be rejected, but when an article it is to be retained. When, however, as in the case of the French *Du, Des*, the two are joined, it is necessary to retain the preposition. This also applies to the case of the Italian *Della,* which is often rejected by cataloguers. English Names are, however, to be arranged under the prefixes

De			*De Quincey.*
Dela	} as {		*Delabeche.*
Van			*Van Mildert.*

because these prefixes are meaningless in English and form an integral part of the name.

6.—Proper Names, with the prefix St., as *St. Albans, St. John,* to be arranged in the alphabet as if written in full *Saint.* When the word *Saint* represents a ceremonial title as in the case of St. Alban, St. Giles, and St. Augustine, these names to be arranged under the letters A and G respectively; but the places St. Albans, St. Giles's, and St. Augustines will be found under the prefix *Saint.* The prefixes M' and Mc to be arranged as if written in full *Mac.*

7.—Peers to be arranged under their titles, by which alone in most cases they are known, and not under their family names, except in such a case as Horace Walpole, who is almost unknown by his title of Earl of Orford, which came to him late in life. Bishops, Deans, etc., to be always under their family names.

8.—Foreign compound names to be arranged under the first name, as *Lacaze Duthiers,* English compound names under the last, except in such cases as *Royston-Pigott,* where the first name is a true surname. The first name in a foreign compound is, as a rule, the surname, but the first name in an English compound is usually a mere Christian name.

9.—An Adjective frequently to be preferred to a substantive as a catch-word, for instance, when it contains the point of the compounds, as *Alimentary* Canal, *English* History. Also when the compound forms a distinctive name, as *Soane* Museum.

10.—The entries to be as short as is consistent with intelligibility, but the insertion of names without *specification of the cause of reference* to be avoided, except in particular cases. The extent of the references, when more than one page, to be marked by giving the first and last pages.

11.—Short entries to be repeated under such headings as are likely to be required, in place of a too frequent use of cross references. These, references, however, to be made from cognate headings, as *Cerebral* to *Brain* and *vice versa,* where the subject matter is different.

12.—In the case of Journals and Transactions brief abstracts of the contents of the several articles or papers to be drawn up and arranged in the alphabetical index under the heading of the article.

13.—Authorities quoted or referred to in a book to be indexed under each author's name, the titles of his works being separately set out, and the word ' quoted ' added in italics.

14.—When the indexed page is large, or contains long lists of names, it is to be divided into four sections, referred to respectively as *a, b, c, d*; thus if a page contains 64 lines, 1-16 will be *a*, 17-32 *b*, 33-48 *c*, 49-64 *d*. If in double columns, the page is still to be divided into four : *a* and *b* forming the upper and lower halves of the first column, and *c* and *d* the upper and lower halves of the second column.

15.—When a work is in more than one volume, the number of the volume is to be specified by small Roman numerals. In the case of long sets, such as the *Gentleman's Magazine*, a special Arabic numeral for indicating the volume distinct from the page numeral may be employed with advantage.

16.—Entries which refer to complete chapters or distinct papers, to be printed in small capitals.

17.—Headings to be printed in a marked type. A dash, instead of indentation, to be used as a mark of repetition. The dash to be kept for entries exactly similar, and the word to be repeated when the second differs in any way from the first. The proper name to be repeated when that of a different person. In the case of joint authors, the Christian names or initials of the first, whose surname is arranged in the alphabet, to be in parentheses, but the Christian names of the second to be in the natural order, as *Smith* (John) and Alexander *Brown*, not *Smith* (John) and *Brown* (Alexander).

The above rules do not apply to Subject Indexes, and in certain cases may need modification in accordance with the special character of the work to be indexed. In all cases specimens of the index must be seen by the Committee before it is finally put in hand.

PRELIMINARY LIST OF ENGLISH INDEXES.

IMMEDIATELY on the formation of the Index Society, Mr. Peacock suggested the publication of a List of such Indexes as have been published in separate volumes, and his suggestion was accepted as one that ought to be carried out. The difficulty then arose as to what constituted an Index ; for instance, many actual Indexes are not so called, and such books as the *Index Expurgatorius* are not really Indexes at all. It was also found that the list would be very extensive and would take up considerable time in compilation. Under these circumstances I proposed to add to my account of Index work a preliminary list of such Indexes as came in my way, and indulgence is asked for the following catalogue, as it is a mere skeleton of one division of the subject. I shall be greatly obliged if readers will send me notice of Foreign Indexes as well as of English ones not mentioned here, so that materials for a full catalogue to be prepared hereafter may be gathered together.

I have been greatly assisted in the compilation of this list by Messrs. Gomme, Peacock, and Solly. Since the first publication I have received much highly appreciated aid from Messrs. Ashbee, Brightwell, and Clements, and from Drs. Crompton, J. B. Hamilton, and Francis H. Brown of Boston, U.S., and from several other kind friends, who sent me titles of Indexes that had escaped my notice. Prof. Justin Winsor was good enough to send me a delightful little volume of 134 pages, entitled, A Handbook for Readers (for the Boston Public Library), which contains a list of Indexes. I have taken out a few of the titles of those which I have been unable to see, and have prefixed a star (*) to them.

SCHEME OF ARRANGEMENT.

CONCORDANCES, &c.

Bible.—A Concordance, that is to saie, a worke wherein by the ordre of the letters of the A B C ye maie redely finde any worde conteigned in the whole Bible, so often as it is there expressed or mencioned . . . anno 1550. [at end] Richardus Grafton, typographus Regius excudebat, Mense Iulii. A. M.D.L. folio.

Dedicated to Edward VI. by the author, John Marbeck. title, 4 preliminary leaves, ff. 1–35, after which the leaves are not numbered. (Sign. a. 1 to vvv. 6 in sixes. Woodcut of Henry VIII in council, 1 leaf.)

——— A briefe and Compendiouse table, in a maner of a Concordaunce openyng the waye to the principall histories of the whole Bible, and the most comon articles grounded and comprehended in the newe Testament and olde, in maner as amply as doeth the great Concordauce of the Bible. Gathered and set furth by Henry Bullynger, Leo Jude, Conrade Pellicane, and by the other Ministers of the Churche of Tygurie. And nowe first imprinted in Englyshe. D M L . . . . London for Gwalter Lynne 1550. Sm. 8vo. A to T 2 in eights.

R. F. Hervey published a Concordance in 1579, which went through several editions; C. Cotton published one in 1622 also frequently reprinted; J. Downame one in 1632 of which there are later editions; and Robert Wickens one at Oxford in 1655. The "Cambridge" Concordance of Samuel Newman (1650),

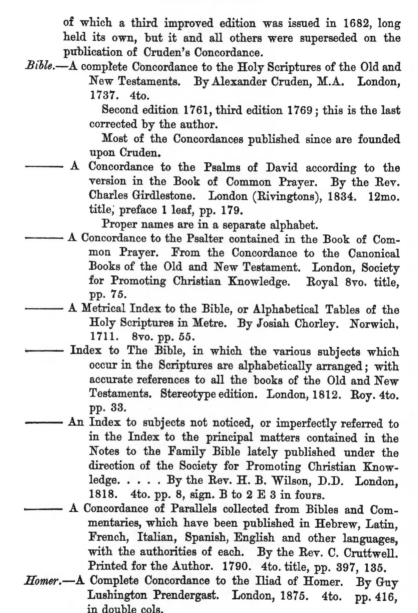

of which a third improved edition was issued in 1682, long
held its own, but it and all others were superseded on the
publication of Cruden's Concordance.

Bible.—A complete Concordance to the Holy Scriptures of the Old and
New Testaments. By Alexander Cruden, M.A.   London,
1737.   4to.

Second edition 1761, third edition 1769; this is the last
corrected by the author.

Most of the Concordances published since are founded
upon Cruden.

——— A Concordance to the Psalms of David according to the
version in the Book of Common Prayer.   By the Rev.
Charles Girdlestone.   London (Rivingtons), 1834.   12mo.
title, preface 1 leaf, pp. 179.

Proper names are in a separate alphabet.

——— A Concordance to the Psalter contained in the Book of Common Prayer.   From the Concordance to the Canonical
Books of the Old and New Testament.   London, Society
for Promoting Christian Knowledge.   Royal 8vo. title,
pp. 75.

——— A Metrical Index to the Bible, or Alphabetical Tables of the
Holy Scriptures in Metre.   By Josiah Chorley.   Norwich,
1711.   8vo. pp. 55.

——— Index to The Bible, in which the various subjects which
occur in the Scriptures are alphabetically arranged; with
accurate references to all the books of the Old and New
Testaments.   Stereotype edition.   London, 1812.   Roy. 4to.
pp. 33.

——— An Index to subjects not noticed, or imperfectly referred to
in the Index to the principal matters contained in the
Notes to the Family Bible lately published under the
direction of the Society for Promoting Christian Knowledge. . . . . By the Rev. H. B. Wilson, D.D.   London,
1818.   4to. pp. 8, sign. B to 2 E 3 in fours.

——— A Concordance of Parallels collected from Bibles and Com-
mentaries, which have been published in Hebrew, Latin,
French, Italian, Spanish, English and other languages,
with the authorities of each.   By the Rev. C. Cruttwell.
Printed for the Author. 1790. 4to. title, pp. 397, 135.

Homer.—A Complete Concordance to the Iliad of Homer.   By Guy
Lushington Prendergast.   London, 1875.   4to.   pp. 416,
in double cols.

Keble.—A Concordance to "The Christian Year." Oxford and London, 1871. 12mo. pp. 524.

Liturgy.—A Concordance to the Liturgy or Book of Common Prayer, etc., according to the use of the United Church of England and Ireland. By the Rev. J. Green, D.D., Vicar of St. Neot's, Hunts. London, 1851. 12mo. pp. x, 431.

Milton.—A Verbal Index to Milton's Paradise Lost, adapted to every edition but the first, which was published in ten books only. London, 1741. 12mo.

——— A Complete Concordance to the Poetical Works of Milton. By Guy Lushington Prendergast, Madras Civil Service. Madras (Pharaoh & Co.) 1857. 4to. title, 1 preliminary leaf, pp. 416.

    Originally published in 12 parts.

——— A Complete Concordance to the Poetical Works of John Milton. By Charles Dexter Cleveland, LL.D. London (Sampson Low, Son & Marston), 1867. Sm. 8vo. pp. viii, 308.

    The Rev. H. J. Todd compiled a verbal Index to the whole of Milton's Poetry which was appended to the second edition of his life of the Poet (1809).

Pope.—A Concordance to the Works of Alexander Pope. By Edwin Abbott, with an Introduction by Edwin A. Abbott, D.D. London (Chapman & Hall), 1875. Royal 8vo. pp. xviii, 366.

Shakespeare.—An Index to the remarkable passages and words made use of by Shakespeare, calculated to point out the different meanings to which the words are applied. By Samuel Ayscough. London, 1790. Royal 8vo.

    Reprinted Dublin 1791 and London 1827 in demy 8vo.

——— A Complete Verbal Index to the Plays of Shakspeare, adapted to all the editions, comprehending every substantive, adjective, verb, participle, and adverb used by Shakespeare; with a distinct reference to every individual passage in which each word occurs. By Francis Twiss. London, 1805. 2 vols. 8vo.

——— The Complete Concordance to Shakspere: being a verbal Index to all the passages in the dramatic works of the Poet. By Mrs. Cowden Clarke. London (C. Knight & Co.) 1845. Royal 8vo. pp. viii, 860.

——— Shakespeare-Lexicon : a Complete Dictionary of all the English words, phrases and constructions in the works of the poet. By Dr. Alexander Schmidt. (Berlin and London), 1874. 2 vols. royal 8vo.

Shakespeare.—A Concordance to Shakespeare's Poems: an Index to every word therein contained. By Mrs. Horace Howard Furness.

> " To your audit comes
> Their distract parcels in combined sums."

Philadelphia (J. B. Lippincott & Co.), 1874. pp. iv, 422.

—— A Hand-Book Index to the Works of Shakespeare, including references to the phrases, manners, customs, proverbs, songs, particles, etc., which are used or alluded to by the great Dramatist. By J. O. Halliwell, Esq., F. R. S. London (J. E. Adlard), 1866. 8vo. pp. vi; contents 1 leaf, pp. 551. Only fifty copies printed.

Tennyson.—A Concordance of the entire works of Alfred Tennyson, P.L., D.C.L., F.R.S. By D. Barron Brightwell. London (Moxon), 1869. 8vo. p. xiv, 477.

—— Concordance to the works of Alfred Tennyson, Poet Laureate. London (Strahan & Co.), 1870. pp. 542.

" The Holy Grail," etc., is indexed separately.

—— An Index to " In Memoriam." London (E. Moxon & Co.), 1862. 12mo. pp. iv, 40.

Watts.—A Complete Index to Dr. Watts' Psalms. By D. Guy, of Rye in Sussex. 1774. 12mo.

Sigs. B to Y 4.

INDEXES OF PARTICULAR BOOKS.

Alison's Europe.—History of Europe from 1815 to 1852, by Sir Archibald Alison, Bart. Index. Edinburgh (Blackwood), 1859. 8vo. title, pp. 319. In one alphabet.

Blomefield's Norfolk.—Index Nominum; being an Index of Christian and Surnames (with arms), mentioned in Blomefield's History of Norfolk, arranged in alphabetical order. By John Nurse Chadwick. King's Lynn (published for the author), 1862. Royal 8vo. pp. 348.

This Index refers to the octavo edition.

Buffon's Natural History—Index to Buffon's Planches enluminees. By Thomas Pennant. 1786. 4to.

Burke's Landed Gentry.—Index of family names in Burke's Genealogical and Heraldic Dictionary of the Landed Gentry—

fourth edition 1863, in Bridger's *Index to Pedigrees* 1867, pp. 178–258.

Burton's Scotland.—The History of Scotland from Agricola's Invasion to the Extinction of the last Jacobite Insurrection. By John Hill Burton, Historiographer Royal for Scotland. Second edition. Index volume. London and Edinburgh (William Blackwood & Sons), 1873. 8vo. pp. 100, in double columns.

Carlyle.—A General Index to the People's edition of Thomas Carlyle's Works. London (Chapman & Hall), 1874. 12mo. pp. 201.

Mr. Carlyle's vehement denunciation of books without indexes is well known, and his sincerity is proved by this careful compilation.

Dugdale's York.—Index to the Visitation of the County of Yorke begun A.D. 1665 and finished A.D. 1666 by William Dugdale, Esq. Norroy King of Armes. Compiled by George J. Armytage. Printed by private subscription. London, 1872. 8vo. title, preface 1 leaf, pp. 40.

In one alphabet, with a list of pedigrees in order of pages appended. Dugdale's Visitation was printed by the Surtees Society in 1859 (vol. 36, their publications).

Encyclopædias.—The Encyclopædia Britannica, or Dictionary of Arts, Sciences and General Literature. Eighth edition. Index. [By James Duncan.] Edinburgh, 1860. Pp. vii, 232. In one alphabet.

—— Encyclopædia Metropolitana, or Universal Dictionary of Knowledge . . . Index. London, 1845. 4to. pp. iv, 370. In one alphabet.

—— The English Cyclopædia. Synoptical Index to the four divisions of Geography, Biography, Natural History, Arts and Sciences. London, 1862. 4to. pp. iv, 166.

Arranged in four columns.

—— General and Analytical Index to the American Encyclopædia. By T. J. Conant, D.D., assisted by his daughter Blandina. New York (Appleton & Co.), 1878. pp. viii, 810. 4to.

Highly praised in *Library Journal*, vol. iii. No. 8, p. 303.

* —— Index to Appleton's Annual Cyclopædia, vols. 1–10.

Criticised adversely in *Library Journal*, vol. ii. p. 296.

Essayists.—A General Index to the Spectators, Tatlers and Guardians. 1757. Second edition. London (W. Owen), 1760. 12mo. unpaged. In one alphabet.

—— The British Essayists; with prefaces, historical and biographical, by A. Chalmers, F.S.A. Vol. 38. General Index. London, 1823. 12mo. title, pp. 277. In one alphabet.

Gmelin's Chemistry.—Index to Gmelin's Handbook of Chemistry. By Henry Watts. London, 1872. 8vo. title, pp. 331. In one alphabet.

Holme's Armory.—Index of the Names of Persons contained in the Academy of Armory and Blazon, by Randle Holme; printed at Chester in one volume folio, 1688. London (R. Triphook), 1821. Folio, title, pp. 46.

Only 50 copies printed. In one alphabet, and contains names of places as well as of persons.

Howell's State Trials.—General Index to the Collection of State Trials, compiled by T. B. Howell and T. J. Howell. By David Jardine. London, 1828. 8vo. title, advertisement 1 leaf, pp. 345.

Part 1, Names; Part 2, Miscellaneous Contents. Appended is "A Table of Parallel References from Howell's State Trials to the folio edition by Hargrave." The references are given as 15 *vol.* instead of *vol.* 15.

Hume's England.—Biographical Index to the History of England; consisting of an Alphabetical Arrangement of all the titles and proper names of persons in Hume's History of England, with Biographical Articles attached. By the Rev. S. Y. McMasters, LL.D. Alton (printed at the Courier Office), 1854. pp. 672.

Madox's Exchequer.—A compleat Index to Mr. Madox's History of the Exchequer, serving as a Glossary to explain uncommon words, to illustrate the original of families and customs, and the antiquities of the several counties in England. London, Printed for Francis Gosling at the Crown and Mitre against Fetter Lane, Fleet Street, 1741. Folio, unpaged, sheets A to Hhh 1, in twos.

This Index was made by the editor of Madox's *Baronia Anglica*, 1741, and was issued with that work. It was reprinted in the second edition of the History of the Exchequer. 2 vols. 4to. 1769. In one alphabet.

Oke & Stone.—A Pocket Index to Oke and Stone. By an Essex Justice [Andrew Johnston]. Gloucester (John Bellows), 1877. 12mo. pp. vii, 56.

This is an Index to "Oke's Magisterial Synopsis: a Practical Guide for Magistrates, their Clerks, Solicitors and Constables. Twelfth edition by T. W. Saunders.

London, 1876." 2 vols. 8vo. And to "The Justice's Manual or Guide to the ordinary duties of a Justice of the Peace, by the late Samuel Stone, the eighteenth edition edited by George B. Kennett. London, 1876." 8vo.

There is no clue in this Index to the titles of the books indexed.

Parliamentary History.—A General Index to the twenty-three volumes of the Parliamentary or Constitutional History of England. London (W. Sandby), 1761. 8vo. pp. 712.

Pennant's London.—Copious Index to Pennant's Account of London. By T. Downes. 1814. 4to. pp. 52, in double columns.

Pictorial History.—Index to the Pictorial History of England, forming a complete chronological key to the civil and military events, the lives of remarkable persons and the progress of the country in religion, government, industry, arts and sciences, literature, manners, and social economy. By H. C. Hamilton. London (Orr & Co.), 1850. Roy. 8vo. pp. iv, 280.

In one alphabet. Dates are largely introduced into the references.

Richardson's Novels.—A Collection of the moral and instructive sentiments, maxims, cautions, and reflexions contained in the Histories of Pamela, Clarissa and Sir Charles Grandison, digested under proper heads, with references to the volume and page, both in octavo and twelves, in the respective histories. London (S. Richardson), 1755. 12mo. pp. x, 410.

There is a separate alphabet for each novel.

Southcott's Writings.—A General Index to the Writings of Joanna Southcott, the Prophetess. London, no date. 8vo. pp. 33.

—— Index to the Divine and Spiritual Writings of Joanna Southcott. By Philip Pullen. London, 1815. 8vo. pp. 240.

Strype's Works.—A General Index to the Historical and Biographical Works of John Strype, A.M. [By the Rev. R. French Lawrence.] Oxford (Clarendon Press), 1828. 2 vols. 8vo. Vol. 1, pp. iv, 406; Vol. 2, title, pp. 404.

In one alphabet.

Tytler's Scotland.—History of Scotland. By Patrick Fraser Tytler. Third edition. Index. Edinburgh (Black), 1850. 8vo. title, pp. 128. In one alphabet.

Warton's English Poetry.—An Index to the History of English
Poetry. By Thomas Warton, B.D. London, 1806.
4to.

In double cols. Six separate Indexes, viz. vol 1, pp. 21.
Dissertation prefixed to vol. 1, 10 pp. vol. 2, pp. 20.
vol. 3, pp. 27. Gesta Romanorum (prefixed to vol. 3),
pp. 6. Fragment of the fourth vol. pp. 6.

Wellington Despatches.—The Index to the Despatches of F. M. the
Duke of Wellington. By Lieut.-Colonel Gurwood.
London, 1839. 8vo. pp. 235, in double cols.

Wesley's Journals.—A complete and classified Index (to suit all
editions) of the Journals of the Rev. John Wesley, M.A.
By the Rev. Henry Skewes, M.A. London (Elliott
Stock, 62 Paternoster Row, E.C.), 1872. 8vo.

Contents, one page; Index of Places, pp. 1–38; Index
of Persons, pp. 39–43; Index of Books, pp. 44–48;
Miscellaneous Index, pp. 49–64.

INDEXES OF ATLASES.

Adam.—A Geographical Index, being a Supplement to the Summary
of Ancient and Modern Geography. By Alexander Adam,
LL.D. Edinburgh, 1795. 8vo.
Sigs. A to S 3 in double cols.

Arrowsmith.—Index to the Eton Comparative Atlas of Ancient and
Modern Geography. New and improved edition. London,
1831. Large 8vo. pt. 1, pp. 90, pt. 2, pp. 86.

Cary.—Cary's English Atlas. An Index . . . London. Folio, pp. 40.
No title-page.

Hall.—An Alphabetical Index to all the names contained in a new
General Atlas of fifty-three Maps. Constructed from
new drawings and engraved by Sidney Hall. London
(Longmans), 1831. Roy. 8vo. title, pp. 360.

Johnston.—Index Geographicus, being a List alphabetically arranged
of the principal places on the Globe, with the countries
and sub-divisions of the countries in which they are
situated and their latitudes and longitudes. Compiled
specially with reference to Keith Johnston's Royal Atlas,
but applicable to all modern atlases and maps. Edinburgh
(Blackwood), 1864. Roy. 8vo. pp. iv, 676.

Ordnance Survey.—Index to the Ordnance Survey of England, Scotland and Ireland. folio.

Useful Knowledge Society.—Index to the Maps of the Society for the Promotion of Useful Knowledge. 1844.

INDEXES TO PUBLICATIONS OF SOCIETIES.

*American Pharmaceutical Association.—Proceedings. Index, vol. 1–8, 1852–59, with the Proceedings for 1862. Index, vol. 9– 17, 1860–69, with the Proceedings for 1872.

Asiatic Society of Bengal.—Index to the first eighteen volumes of the Asiatic Researches, or Transactions of the Society, instituted in Bengal for inquiring into the History and Antiquities, the Arts, Sciences and Literature of Asia. Calcutta, 1835. 4to. pp. vi, 228.

——— Index to volumes 19 and 20 of the Asiatic Researches and to the Journal of the Asiatic Society of Bengal. Calcutta, 1856. 8vo. pp. iv, 274. In one alphabet, with 4 Appendixes— A. Index to Numismatic Papers, etc. By G. H. Freeling. B. Sykes's List of Ancient Inscriptions. C. Index to Geological Papers. By H. Piddington. D. Table of Indian Coal. By J. Prinsep; and Supplementary Index.

British Archæological Association. — The Journal of the British Archæological Association. General Index to Volumes 1 to 30. By Walter De Gray Birch. London, 1875. 8vo. pp. 225.

In one alphabet. A Table of the Contents of each volume is appended.

British Association.—Index to Reports and Transactions of the British Association for the Advancement of Science, from 1831 to 1860 inclusive. London, 1864. 8vo. pp. iv, 363.

In six separate alphabets, viz.—*Reports :* Index of Authors, of Subjects, and of Places; *Sections :* Index of Authors, of Subjects, and of Places.

Chemical Society.—Index to the first twenty-five volumes of the Journal of the Chemical Society, 1848-1872 ; and to the Memoirs and Proceedings, 1841-1847. Compiled by Henry Watts, Editor of the Journal. London, 1874. 8vo. pp. 268.

In two parts. 1, Index of Names; 2, Index of Subjects.

Chetham Society.—General Index to the Remains, Historical and Literary, published by the Chetham Society, Vols. 1—30. By C. S. Simms. Manchester, 1863. 4to. pp. viii, 168, 11 leaves of Indexes to separate volumes.

Geological Society.—A Classified Index to the Transactions, Proceedings and Quarterly Journal of the Geological Society of London, including all the memoirs and notices to the end of 1855. By George Wareing Ormerod. London (Taylor & Francis, 1858. 8vo. pp. vii, 149.

New edition to the end of 1868, with Supplement to the end of 1875. 8vo.

Geological Survey of India.—Contents and Index of the first ten volumes of the Records of the Geological Survey of India, 1868 to 1877. Calcutta, 1878. Roy. 8vo. pp. 23.

Guy's Hospital.—General Index to the first and second series of the Guy's Hospital Reports. London (J. Churchill), 1856. 8vo. pp. xlii, 106, 58. In one alphabet.

General Index to the third series . . . including the first ten volumes (1854–1864). 8vo. pp. 26. General Index . . . for Vols. 11 to 20 (1865–1875), pp. 591-624 of Vol. 20.

Horticultural Society.—General Index to the first and second series of the Transactions of the Horticultural Society of London. 4to. pp. cxxxviii. No title-page.

In one alphabet.

Institution of Civil Engineers.—Minutes of Proceedings of the Institution of Civil Engineers. General Index, Volumes 1 to 20. Sessions 1837 to 1860–61. London, 1865. 8vo. pp. iv, 367.

In one alphabet.

—— General Index, Volumes 21 to 30. Sessions 1861-62 to 1869-70. London, 1871. 8vo. pp. iv, 206.

In one alphabet.

Institution of Mechanical Engineers.—General Index to Proceedings, 1847-1873. Birmingham. 8vo. title, pp. 220.

In one alphabet.

Lancashire & Cheshire.—Historic Society of Lancashire and Cheshire. Index to the first and second series of the Society's Transactions, comprising Vols. 1—24 inclusive, prepared by the Rev. A. Hume. Liverpool (T. Brakell), 1874. 8vo. pp. iv, 47.

In three parts. 1, Tables of the Contents of each

volume; 2, Alphabetical List of Authors; 3, Alphabetical List of Subjects.

Linnean Society.—General Index to the Transactions of the Linnean Society of London. Vols. 1 to 25. London, 1867. 4to. pp. iv, 107. In two parts. 1, Index to Papers; 2, Index of Genera and Species. A continuation of the Index, from Vol. 26 to 30, has since been published.

Liverpool Lit. & Phil. Soc.—Index to Papers contained in the Proceedings of the Literary and Philosophical Society of Liverpool. Vols. 1–25. 1844–71. Compiled by Alfred Morgan, Honorary Librarian. Liverpool (D. Marples), 1871. 8vo. pp. 28.

Manchester Statistical Society.—Index to the Transactions of the Manchester Statistical Society from 1853–4 to 1874–5. By Thomas Read Wilkinson, President of the Society, 1875–6. Manchester, 1876. 8vo. pp. 82.

Contains 1, Table of Contents; 2, List of Tables; 3, Alphabetical Index; 4, Alphabetical List of Writers.

In two parts. 1, Index of Subjects; 2, Index of Authors.

New Zealand Institute.—Transactions and Proceedings of the New Zealand Institute. Index, vols. 1 to 8. Edited by James Hector. Wellington, 1877. 8vo. title, pp. 44.

Divided into—1, Index of Authors; 2, Index of Subjects; 3, Appendix.

North of England Institute of Mining and Mechanical Engineers.—General Index to the Transactions. roy. 8vo.

Parker Society.—A General Index to the Publications of the Parker Society. Compiled for the Parker Society, by Henry Gough, of the Middle Temple. Cambridge (University Press), 1855. 8vo. pp. viii, 811. In one alphabet.

Pathological Society.—A General Index to the first fifteen volumes of the Transactions of the Pathological Society of London; with a List of Authors and a Classified List of Subjects. Compiled by T. Holmes. London, 1864. 8vo. pp. vii, 147.

In two parts. 1, Index of Subjects; 2, Index of Authors.

—— General Index to the Transactions of the Pathological Society of London, from Vols. 16 to 25, 1865-74. [By B. R. Wheatley.] London, 1875. 8vo. pp. v, 134.

In one alphabet.

Royal Agricultural Society.—General Index to the first series of the Journal of the Royal Agricultural Society of England, Volumes 1 to 25   London, 1865.   8vo. pp. 214.

In one alphabet.

——— General Index to the second series of the Journal of the Royal Agricultural Society of England, Volumes 1 to 10. London, 1875.   8vo. pp. 134.

In one alphabet.

Royal Astronomical Society.—A General Index to the first thirty-eight volumes of the Memoirs of the Royal Astronomical Society. London, 1871.   8vo. title, pp. 54.

In one alphabet.

——— A General Index to the first twenty-nine volumes of the Monthly Notices of the Royal Astronomical Society, comprising the Proceedings of the Society from February 9, 1827, to the end of the session 1868-69.   London, 1870. 8vo. title, pp. 212.   In one alphabet.

Royal Geographical Society.—General Index to the Contents of the first ten volumes of the London Geographical Journal. Compiled by J. R. Jackson. London, 1844. 8vo. pp. iv, 216.

In one alphabet.   Prefixed are Lists of the Papers and Maps arranged geographically.

——— General Index to the second ten volumes of the Journal of the Royal Geographical Society.   Compiled by George Smith Brent; edited by Dr. Norton Shaw. London, 1853. 8vo. pp. 116.   Compiled on the same plan as the first Index.

Royal Irish Academy.—An Index to the Transactions of the Royal Irish Academy from its incorporation in 1786 to the present time [Vols. 1 to 11].   By Nicholas Carlisle. London, 1813. 4to. pp. viii, 316.

In two parts.   1, Index of the Names of Persons; 2, Index of the Names of Places and of Subjects.

Royal Medical & Chir. Soc.—General Index to the first thirty-three volumes of the Medico-Chirurgical Transactions, published by the Royal Medical and Chirurgical Society of London. [By Dr. John Hennen.] London, 1851. 8vo. pp. lxxx, 236.

In one alphabet.   Prefixed is a list of the contents of each volume, and a list of engravings.

——— General Index to the first fifty-three volumes of the Medico-Chirurgical Transactions, published by the Royal Medical and Chirurgical Society of London.   [By B. R. Wheatley.] London, 1871. 8vo. pp. viii, 355.   In one alphabet.

Royal Society.—A General Index to the Philosophical Transactions, from the first to the end of the seventieth volume. By Paul Henry Maty, M.A., F.R.S., Under Librarian to the British Museum. London, 1787. 4to. pp. iv, 801.

In two alphabets—1, of the Matter; 2, of the Writers.

—— A continuation to the Alphabetical Index of the Matter contained in the Philosophical Transactions of the Royal Society of London, from vol. 71 (1781) to 110 (1820) inclusive [including a continuation of the Index of Writers]. London, 1821. 4to. pp. iv, 225.

—— A continuation to the Alphabetical Index . . . . from vol. 111 (1821) to 120 (1830). London, 1833. 4to. pp. 101.

—— An Index to the Anatomical, Medical, Chirurgical and Physiological Papers contained in the Transactions of the Royal Society of London, from the commencement of that work to the end of the year 1813, chronologically and alphabetically arranged. Westminster (M. Stace), 1814. 4to. pp. iv, 101. In two divisions.

—— Table des Memoires imprimés dans les Transactions Philosophiques de la Société Royale de Londres ; depuis 1665 jusques en 1735, rangees par ordre chronologique, par ordre des matieres, et par noms d'auteurs; par M. de Bremond. Paris, 1739. 4to. title, 3 preliminary leaves, pp. v, 297, 461, lxxvi.

Royal United Service Institution.—Index of the Lectures and Papers contained in vols. 1–10 of the Journal of the Royal United Service Institution, and also the names of their Authors. London, 1868. 8vo. pp. 47. Index, vols. 11–20. London, 1878. 8vo. pp. 75. In two alphabets.

Society of Antiquaries.—An Index to the first fifteen volumes of Archæologia, or Miscellaneous Tracts relating to Antiquity ; printed by order of the Society of Antiquaries of London. [By Nicholas Carlisle.] London, 1809. 4to. pp. iv. 290.

In two parts—1, Index of Names of Persons ; 2, Index of Names of Places and of Subjects.

—— An Index to Archæologia, from volume 16 to volume 30 inclusive; published by the Society of Antiquaries of London. [By Nicholas Carlisle.] London, 1844. 4to. pp. iv, 309. In one alphabet.

A new and complete Index to the whole set of the *Archæologia*, from volume 1 to 40, is now being prepared.

Society of Arts.—An Analytical Index to the first twenty-five volumes of the Transactions of the Society instituted at London for the encouragement of Arts, Manufactures, and Commerce, London, 1807. 8vo. pp. 142.

———— Vol. 26 to 40. 1823. 8vo. pp. 47.

———— Vol. 41 to 50. 1836. 8vo. pp. xxxvi.

———— The Journal of the Society of Arts and of the Institutions in Union. Index to Vols. 1–10. London, 1863. Roy. 8vo. pp. lvii. In one alphabet.

———— Vols. 11–20. 1873. Roy. 8vo.

Statistical Society.—Journal of the Statistical Society of London. General Index to the first fifteen volumes. [By B. R. Wheatley.] London, 1854. 8vo. pp. vii, 198. In one alphabet.

——— General Index to Volumes 16—25 (1853-1862), in continuation of the General Index to the first fifteen volumes. London, 1863. 8vo. pp. iv, 135. In one alphabet.

——— General Index to Volumes 26—35 (1863-72) in continuation of the General Indexes to Volumes 1—15 (1834-52) and 16—25 (1853-62). London, 1874. 8vo. pp. vii, 152. In one alphabet.

Sussex Arch. Society.—Sussex Archæological Collections, relating to the History and Antiquities of the County, published by the Sussex Archæological Society. General Index to Vols. 1 to 25. By Henry Campkin, F.S A. Lewes, 1874. 8vo. pp. viii, 423. In one alphabet.

Yorkshire, &c.—An Index to the first eight volumes of Reports and Papers read at the Meetings of the Architectural Societies of Yorkshire, Lincolnshire, Northampton, Bedfordshire, Worcestershire and Leicestershire during the years 1850-66, containing an Analysis of each Paper, with an Introduction by the Rev. George Rowe, M.A. Lincoln (Brookes and Viber), n.d. 8vo.

Zoological Society —Proceedings of the Zoological Society of London. Index, 1830-1847. London, 1866. 8vo. pp. iv, 190.
    In two parts. 1, List of Contributors; 2, Index of Species.

——— Index, 1848-1860. London, 1863. 8vo. pp. iv, 304.
    In three parts. 1, List of Contributors; 2, List of Illustrations; 3, Index of Species.

——— Proceedings of the Scientific Meetings of the Zoological

Society of London. Index, 1861-1870. London, 1872. 8vo. pp. iv. 481.

In two parts. 1, List of Contributors; 2, Index of Species.

INDEXES OF PERIODICALS.

All the Year Round.—General Index to the first twenty volumes of All the Year Round. 1868. pp. 32, in three columns.
Under the headings of Miscellaneous Articles, Poetry, Tales.

*American Almanac.—Indexes, ten years each, in vols. 1839, 1849, 1859.

American Journal.—The American Journal of Science and Arts. Conducted by Prof. Silliman and Benj. Silliman, jun. Volume 50. General Index to forty-nine volumes. New Haven, 1847. 8vo. pp. xviii, 348.
In one general alphabet, with a Supplement of omitted references and a Register of Plates, Maps and other Illustrations.

—— Second Series. Vol. 10 (1850) contains Index for Vols. 1—10; Vol. 20 (1855) for Vols. 11—20; Vol. 30 (1860) for Vols. 21—30; Vol. 40 (1865) for Vols. 31—40; Vol. 50 (1870) for Vols. 41—50.

—— Third Series. Vol. 10 (1875) contains Index for Vols. 1-10.

*American Journal of Pharmacy.—General Index, 1825-1870.

*American Jurist and Law Magazine. —In vols. 10 and 20.

Annual Register.—A General Index to the Annual Register; or, A Summary View of the History of Europe, Domestic Occurrences . . . . . from 1758 to 1780, both inclusive. (The second edition, 1784.) The third edition. London (Rivington), 1799. 8vo. unpaged. Half-title, "Index to Dodsley's Annual Register, Vol. 1, 1758 to 1780." Arranged in fourteen alphabets.

—— from 1781 to 1792, both inclusive. London (Rivington), 1799. 8vo. unpaged. Half-title, "Index to Dodsley and Rivington's Annual Register, Vol. 2, 1781 to 1792."
Arranged like the former volume in fourteen alphabets. There is also a General Index under seven heads, from 1758 to 1819. 1826. 8vo. pp. 938.

Assurance Magazine, and Journal of the Institute of Actuaries. General Index to vols. 1–10. By John Nicholson, Assistant Librarian of Lincoln's Inn. London, 1864. 8vo.

Atlantic Monthly. —Index to the Atlantic Monthly, Volumes i–xxxviii. (1857–1876). By Horace E. Scudder. 1. Index of Articles (a) General Articles, (b) Editorial Departments. 2. Index of Authors. Boston (H. O. Houghton & Co.), 1877. 8vo. pp. 106.

    In double columns and interleaved.

Biblical Repertory and Princeton Review.—Index volume from 1825 to 1868. Philadelphia (Peter Walker), 1871.

    This contains also a Retrospect of the history of the Princeton Review, and an Index to Authors, with Biographical Notices.

Bibliotheca Sacra.—Index to the Bibliotheca Sacra, and American Biblical Repertory. Volumes 1 to 13, containing an Index of Subjects and Authors, a Topical Index, and a List of Scripture Texts. By W. F. Draper. Andover (Mass.), 1857.

—————— Index to the Bibliotheca Sacra, volumes 1 to 30. An Index of Scripture Texts and Texts of Greek and Hebrew Words. By W. F. Draper. Andover, 1874.

Blackwood's Magazine.—General Index to Blackwood's Edinburgh Magazine, Vols. 1 to 50. Edinburgh (Blackwood and Sons), 1855. 8vo. title, pp. 588.

    In one alphabet.

Botanical Magazine.—General Indexes to the Plants contained in the first twenty volumes of the Botanical Magazine. London, 1805. 8vo. pp. 53.

    Partly in double cols.

—————— General Indexes to the Plants in the first fifty-three volumes of the Botanical Magazine. By Samuel Curtis. 1828. 8vo.

British & For. Med. Rev.—The British and Foreign Medical Review . . Edited by John Forbes, M.D. Vol. 25, being a General Index to the preceding twenty-four volumes. London (J. Churchill), 1848. 8vo. pp. xi, 303. By Dr. Robert Bower.

    In one alphabet.

British Critic.—A General Index to the first twenty volumes of the British Critic, in two parts. Part 1 contains a List of all the Books Reviewed. Part 2 an Index to the Extracts, Criticisms, etc. London, 1804. 8vo. pp. iii, 386.

—————— A General Index to the British Critic, commencing with the twenty-first and ending with the forty-second or concluding volume of the first series, in two parts. Part 1 contains a List of all the Books Reviewed. Part 2 an Index to the Extracts, Criticisms, etc. London, 1815. 8vo. pp. iv, 343.

Calcutta Review.—Index to the first Fifty Volumes of the Calcutta Review, in two parts. Calcutta (Thos. J. Smith), 1873. 8vo.

>Part. 1. Index to Articles and Books. pp. 196, in double columns. Part 2. Index to Subjects noticed incidentally in the Articles contained in Part 1. pp. 47, in double columns.

Companion to the Almanac.—A complete Index to the Companion to the Almanac, from its commencement in 1828 to 1843 inclusive. London (C. Knight & Co.), 1843. 12mo. title, pp. 561.

>In one alphabet, with a Supplementary Index.

* *Congregational Quarterly,* vol. 1–10.

Dublin Medical Journal.—A General Index to the Dublin Medical Journal, from volume 1 to 28, concluding the first series, from 1832 to 1845 inclusive. 8vo. pp. 127.

>In one alphabet.

Edinburgh Review.—General Index to the Edinburgh Review, from its commencement in October, 1802, to the end of the twentieth volume, published in November, 1812. Edinburgh, 1813. 8vo. pp. v, 515. In one alphabet. Prefixed is an Index of Authors reviewed.

———, from the twenty-first to the fiftieth volumes inclusive (1813–1830). Edinburgh, 1832. 8vo. pp. xxi, 513.

>In one alphabet, with an Index of the Titles of the Articles prefixed.

———, from the fifty-first to the eightieth volumes inclusive (1830–1844). London, 1850. 8vo. pp. 511.

>In one alphabet. Prefixed is an Index of the Titles of the Articles according to the running heads of each.

———, from the eighty-first to the hundred and tenth volumes inclusive (1845–1859). London, 1862. 8vo. pp. 474.

>Same as previous Index.

———, from the hundred and eleventh to the hundred and fortieth volumes inclusive (1860–1874). London, 1876. 8vo. title, pp. 431. Same as previous Index.

Edinburgh Med. and Surg. Journal.—The Edinburgh Medical and Surgical Journal . . . volume twentieth, Index [to the first nineteen volumes]. Edinburgh (A. Constable & Co.), 1824. 8vo. pp. vii, 395.

In one alphabet, to which are added Index of *works reviewed;* and catalogue of Edinburgh Theses, from 1726 to 1823.

Gentleman's Magazine.—A General Index to the first fifty-six volumes of the Gentleman's Magazine, from 1731 to the end of 1786. Compiled by Samuel Ayscough, Clerk, Assistant Librarian of the British Museum. In two volumes. Vol. 1 containing an Index to the Essays, Dissertations, and Historical Passages. London (J. Nichols), 1789. 8vo. pp. iv, 494.

———— Vol. 2, in four parts, containing Indexes to the Poetical Articles, the Names of Persons and Plates, and to the Books and Pamphlets. London (J. Nichols), 1789. 8vo. title, pp. 368.

———— from 1787 to 1818, both inclusive. Vol. 3, in two parts, containing Indexes to the Essays, Dissertations, Transactions and Historical Passages, and to the Poetical Articles. With a prefatory Introduction descriptive of the rise and progress of the Magazine by John Nichols. London (J. Nichols & Son), 1821. 8vo. pp. lxxx, 543.

———— Vol. 4, in five parts, containing Indexes to Books reviewed and Books announced; to the Musical publications; to the Plates; and to the Names of Persons. London (J. Nichols & Son), 1821. 8vo. title, pp. 656.

———— A List of Plates, Maps, etc., in the Gentleman's Magazine from 1731 to 1813 inclusive. London (Machell Stace), 1814. 8vo. pp. iv, 58.

———— A complete List of the Plates and Woodcuts in the Gentleman's Magazine, from 1731 to 1818 inclusive, and an Alphabetical Index thereto. London (J. Nichols & Son), 1821. 8vo. pp. viii, 226.

Hansard's Debates.—General Index to the first and second series of Hansard's Parliamentary Debates, forming a Digest of the recorded Proceedings of Parliament from 1803 to 1830. Edited by Sir John Philippart. London, 1834. Roy. 8vo. pp. v, viii, 743. In several divisions.

Harper's Magazine.—An Index to Harper's New Monthly Magazine, volumes 1 to 50; from June, 1850, to May, 1875. New York (Harper & Brothers), 1875. 8vo.

Arranged in one alphabet. Each alternate page has

been left blank, so that the Index can be continued by any person for a large number of volumes to come. pp. viii, 580 (including the blank pages), in double columns.

A previous Index of vols. 1 to 40 was published in 1870.

Leisure Hour.—Index to the Leisure Hour, vol. 1–25, 1852–76. royal 8vo. pp. 48 in four-columned pages.

London Magazine.—The General Index to twenty-seven volumes of the London Magazine, viz., from 1732 to 1758 inclusive. London, 1760. 8vo. unpaged.

1, Index to the Essays; 2, to the Poetry; 3, of Names; 4, to the Books.

London Med. & Phys. Journal.—A General Index to the London Medical and Physical Journal from Volume 1 to 40 inclusive, containing an analytical Table of their Contents, arranged in alphabetical order, with references to the whole of the cited authorities, under their nominal characters, etc. London (J. Souter), 1820. 8vo. pp. iv, 358.

In one alphabet, with a supplement.

Medico-Chirurgical Review.—General Index to the new series of the Medico-Chirurgical Review, volume 1 to volume 20 inclusive (from June 1, 1824, to June 1, 1834). With an appendix comprising an Index to the series of four annual volumes, from June, 1820, to April, 1824. London (S. Highley), 1834. 8vo. title, pp. 110.

Merchants' Magazine.—A Compendious Index to the Merchants' Magazine and Commercial Review, embracing the first two volumes, from its commencement in July, 1839, to June, 1844, inclusive. New York, 1846.

Monthly Review.—A General Index to the Monthly Review, from its commencement to the end of the seventieth volume. By the Rev. S. Ayscough. In two volumes; Vol. 1 containing a [classified] Catalogue of the books and pamphlets characterized, with the size and price of each article, to which is added a complete Index of the names mentioned in the Catalogue; Vol. 2 containing an Alphabetical Index to all the memorable passages . . . contained in the Monthly Review. London, 1786. 8vo. Vol. 1, pp. xi, 714; Vol. 2, title, pp. 571.

Monthly Review.—A continuation of the General Index to the Monthly Review, commencing at the seventy-first and ending with the eighty-first volume, completing the first series of that work, in two parts. Compiled by the Rev. S. Ayscough. London, 1796. 8vo. pp. iv, 288.

Arranged upon the same plan as the previous Index.

———— A General Index to the Monthly Review, from the commencement of the new series in January, 1790, to the end of the eighty-first volume, completed in December, 1816. In two volumes; Vol. 1 containing a Catalogue of the books and pamphlets . . . . . Vol. 2 containing an Alphabetical Index. London (J. Porter), 1818. Vol. 1, pp. ix, 958; Vol. 2, title, table 1 leaf, pp. 624.

Naturalist's Miscellany.—General Indexes, in Latin and English, to the subjects contained in the twenty-four volumes of the Naturalist's Miscellany. By the late George Shaw, M.D., and Rich. P. Nodder. London, 1813. 8vo. pp. 26, in double cols.

* *New England Historical and Genealogical Register*, vol. 1–15.

New Englander.—Index to the New Englander, vols. 1–19 (1843 to 1861), containing an Index of Authors, a topical index, an index of books noticed and reviewed, and a list of engravings. Vol. 20. New Haven, Conn. (William L. Kingsley, Editor and Proprietor), 1862.

New York Daily Tribune.—Index for 1876. The Tribune Association, New York.

New York Medical Journal.—General Index to the New York Medical Journal, from April, 1865, to June, 1876. By James B. Hunter, M.D. New York (Appleton & Co.), 1877.

New York Times.—Index to the New York Times for 1865. Including the Second Inauguration of President Lincoln, and his Assassination; the Accession of President Johnson; the close of the 38th and the opening of the 39th Congress, and the close of the War of Secession. New York (Henry J. Raymond & Co.), 1866.

* *Niles's Weekly Register*, vol. 1–12, 1811–18.

North American Review.—General Index to the North American Review, from its commencement in 1815 to the end of the 25th volume, 1827. Boston (Gray & Bowen), 1829.

———— New and Complete Index, vol. 1–125, 1815–77. By W. Cushing. Cambridge, Mass., 1878. 8vo. in two parts. 1. Subjects; 2. Writers.

Reviewed in *Library Journal*, vol. iii. No. 9, p. 343.

Notes and Queries.—Notes and Queries. General Index to Series the First, Vols. 1 to 12. [By James Yeowell.] London (Bell and Daldy), 1856. 4to. pp. iv. 146.

——— General Index to Series the Second, Vols. 1 to 12. [By J. Yeowell.] London (Bell & Daldy), 1862. 4to. pp. vi, 160.

——— General Index to Series the Third (1862–1867), Vols. 1 to 12. [By J. Yeowell.] London (Office, 43, Wellington Street), 1868. 4to. pp. iv, 156.

——— General Index to Series the Fourth (1868–1873), Vols. 1 to 12. London (J. Francis), 1874. 4to. title, preface, 1 leaf, pp. 166.

Pharmaceutical Journal.—Index to fifteen volumes of the Pharmaceutical Journal. London (J. Churchill), 1857. 8vo. half title, title, pp. 202, double columns. In one alphabet.

——— Index to twelve volumes of the Pharmaceutical Journal, vol. xvi, Old Series (1856) to vol. ix, Second Series (1868). London, 1869. 8vo. pp. 155, in double cols.

Philosophical Magazine.—General Index to the Philosophical Magazine, or Annals of Chemistry, Mathematics, Astronomy, Natural History and General Science, Volumes 1 to 11 (1827–1832). London (R. Taylor), 1835. 8vo. pp. 50. In one alphabet.

——— General Index to the London and Edinburgh Philosophical Magazine and Journal of Science . . for Volumes 1 to 12 (1832–1838). London (R. & J. E. Taylor), 1839. 8vo. pp. 58. In one alphabet.

Practitioner.—General Index to volumes i–xii. London, 1876. 8vo. pp. 62 in double cols.

Quarterly Journal of Science.—Index to the first twenty volumes of the Quarterly Journal of Science and the Arts. London (J. Murray), 1826. 8vo. title, pp. 218. In one alphabet.

Quarterly Review.—The Quarterly Review, Vol. 20. General Index to the first nineteen volumes. London, 1820. 8vo. pp. xxiv, 514.

In three parts. 1, Personal Names; 2, Subjects; 3, New Publications. Prefixed are Lists of Books and of Authors reviewed.

——— Vol. 40. General Index to Volumes 21 to 39. London, 1831. 8vo. pp. xxxi, 366.

Arranged on the same system as the first Index.

——— Vol. 60. General Index to Volumes 41 to 59. London, 1839. 8vo. title, pp. 612. In one alphabet.

Quarterly Review.—Vol. 80. General Index to Volumes 61 to 79. London, 1850. 8vo. pp. 326. In one alphabet.

—— Vol. 100. General Index to Volumes from 81 to 99 inclusive. London, 1858. 8vo. title, pp. 310. In one alphabet.

—— Vol. 121. General Index to Volumes from 101 to 120 inclusive. London, 1867. 8vo. title, pp. 298. In one alphabet.

Repertory of Arts.—An Analytical Index to the sixteen volumes of the first series of the Repertory of Arts and Manufactures, being a condensed epitome of that work, accompanied by Alphabetical Lists of the Authors and Patentees whose Memoirs and Patents are inserted therein, and of all Patents granted for Inventions from the year 1795 to April, 1802. To which is added a General Index to the first eight volumes of the second series. London, 1806. 8vo. pp. iv, 232, 43.

The first Index is in two alphabets, the second is in one.

**Scribner's Monthly*, vol. 1–10.

Times (The).—An Index to "The Times," and to the topics and events of the year 1862. [By J. Giddings.] London (W. Freeman), 1863. 8vo. pp. vi, 87.

—— An Index to "The Times," and to the topics and events of the year 1863. By J. Giddings. London (S. Palmer), 1864. 8vo. pp. xxvii, 201.

—— Index to "The Times" Newspaper, April, 1865, to June, 1878. London (S. Palmer). 4to. 52 vols.

Commenced in 1865 and continued in quarterly volumes.

Westminster Review.—A General Index to the Westminster Review, from the first to the thirteenth volume inclusive, to which is added an Index of Names. London (R. Heward), 1832. 8vo. half-title, title, pp. 216.

INDEXES TO THE STATUTES.

1215–1714.—The Alphabetical Index to the Statutes of the Realm from Magna Charta to the end of the reign of Queen Anne. London, 1824. folio.

The Chronological Index to the Statutes of the Realm, from Magna Charta to the end of the reign of Queen Anne. London, 1828. folio.

1215–1761.—The Statutes at Large, from Magna Charta to 1761, Vol. 24 being the Index, by Danby Pickering. Cambridge, 1769. 8vo. 2 titles, pp. vii, 633. In one alphabet.

1215–1769.—A Complete Index to the Statutes at Large, from Magna Charta to the tenth year of George III. inclusive, by Owen Ruffhead and another gentleman. London, 1772. 8vo. unpaged. In one alphabet.

1215–1808.—An Index to the Statutes at Large, from Magna Charta to the forty-ninth year of George III. inclusive. By John Raithby, of Lincoln's Inn. In three volumes. London (Eyre & Strahan), 1814. 8vo. unpaged. In one alphabet.

1224–1847.—An Index to the Public Statutes from 9 Hen. III. to 10 & 11 Vict. inclusive (excepting those relating exclusively to Scotland, Ireland, the Colonies and Dependencies). Analytically arranged and affording a synoptical view of the Statute Book. In two parts. Part 1 by Henry Riddell and John Warrington Rogers, of the Middle Temple. London (Benning & Co.), 1848. 8vo. pp. xiv, half title, pp. 406.

1727–1834.—An Analytical Table of the Private Statutes, passed between 1 Geo. II. 1727, and 52 Geo. III. 1812, both inclusive . . . . By George Bramwell, of Lincoln's Inn Fields. London (T. Davison), 1813. 8vo. unpaged.

————— An Analytical Table of the Private Statutes passed between 53 Geo. III. 1813, and 4, 5 Will. IV. 1834. . . Vol. 2. London, 1835. 8vo. unpaged.

1798–1839.—Index to the Local and Personal and Private Acts, 1798–1839, 38 Geo. III.—2 & 3 Vict. By Thomas Vardon. London (Hansards), 1840. 8vo. title, preface 1 leaf, pp. 485. In one alphabet.

1801–1828.—Index to the Public General Statutes of the United Kingdom from January, 1801, to July, 1828. By B. Spiller, Librarian, House of Commons. London (Hansards), 1829. 4to. pp. xxi, ff. 306.

Printed on one side only, the verso of each leaf being left blank for additions. In one alphabet.

1801–1865.—An Index to the Statutes, Public and Private, passed in the several years from the Union with Ireland to the termination of the eighteenth Parliament of the United Kingdom, 41 Geo. III. (1801) to 28 & 29 Vict. (1865). In two parts. Part 1, The Public General Acts, with a chronological list of Acts repealed. Compiled by order of the Select Committee on the Library of the House of Lords, 1867. Folio. Prefatory observations, pp. vii, pp. 703, clxxi.

Part II. The Local and Personal Acts, Local Acts and Private Acts in classes. 1867. Pp. vi, 1033.

An Index to the Statute Law of England, by George Stamp; the third edition brought down to the close of the Session 24 & 25 Vict. (1861) by James Edward Davis. London, 1862. 8vo. pp. xcv, 468.

In one alphabet, with a Table of Titles prefixed.

Chronological Table and Index of the Statutes to 1869. 8vo. 1870. Fourth edition, to the end of the Session of 1877, 40 & 41 Victoria. London, 1878. Roy. 8vo. pp. xi, 842. Containing Table of Variances; Chronological Table; Alphabetical Index and Appendices.

India.—Chronological Table of, and Index to, the Indian Statute-Book from the year 1834, with a General Introduction to the Statute Law of India. By C. D. Field, M.A., LL.D. London (Butterworths), 1870. 4to. pp. vi, 1 leaf, pp. 277.

Ireland.—Index to the Irish Statutes. By Andrew Newton Oulton. 2 vols. with Supplements.

Year Books, etc.—Repertorium Juridicum. An Index to all the cases in the year-books, entries, reports and abridgments in Law and Equity; beginning with Edward I. and continued down to this time. [By Kennett Freeman.] London, 1742. 2 parts, folio.

INDEXES TO THE JOURNALS OF THE HOUSES OF LORDS AND COMMONS.

House of Lords.—Calendar of the Journals of the House of Lords, from the beginning of the reign of Henry VIII. to 30 Aug., 1642, and from 1660 to 21 Jan., 1808. [London, 1810.] Folio, pp. xxiii, 779.

———————— from 21st Jan., 1808, to 14th Nov., 1826. [London]. Folio, pp. vii, 288.

General Index to the Journals of the House of Lords. Vol. 1–10. 1509–1649. [London], 1836. Folio, title, pp. 679.

Vol. 11–19. 1660–1714. [London], 1834. Folio, title, pp. 380.

Vol. 20–35. 1714–1779. Compiled by Thomas Brodie. [London], 1817. Folio, title, pp. 905.

Vol. 36–52. 1780–1819. [London], 1832. Folio, title, pp. 1027.

Vol. 53–64. 1820–1833. [London], 1855. Folio, title, pp. 775.

1833–1863. London, 1865. 2 vols. folio.

House of Commons.—A General Index to the first seven volumes of the Journals of the House of Commons. Compiled by Timothy Cunningham. [London], 1785. Folio, pp. vii, 24 prelim. leaves, pp. 1100. (Vol. 8–11 by Flaxman, vol. 12–17 by Forster, superseded by the next article.)

—— General Index to the Journals of the House of Commons, Vol. 1–17, 1547–1714. By Thomas Vardon and Thomas Erskine May. [London], 1852. Folio. Pp. vii, 1149.

—— A General Index to, or Digest of, seventeen volumes of the Journals of the House of Commons—

Vol. 18–34, 1714–1774. [By E. Moore.] [London], 1778. Folio, unpaged.

Vol. 35–45, 1774–1790. [By S. Dunn.] [London], 1796. Folio, unpaged.

Vol. 46–55, 1790–1800. [By S. Dunn.] [London], 1803. Folio, unpaged.

Vol. 56–75, 1801–1820. By Martin Charles Burney. [London], 1825. Folio.

Vol. 75–92, 1820–1837. By Thomas Vardon. [London], 1839. Folio, pp. xx, 1072.

Vol. 93–107, 1837–1852. By Thomas Vardon. [London], 1857. Folio, pp. viii, 1 leaf, pp. 999.

Ireland.—Index to the Commons' Journals of Ireland.

INDEXES OF PARLIAMENTARY PAPERS.

House of Lords.—A General Index to the Sessional Papers printed by order of the House of Lords or presented by Special Command, 1801–1837. [London], 1839. Folio, title, pp. 370.

—— A General Index to the Sessional Papers printed by order of the House of Lords or presented by Special Command, from the Union with Ireland to the termination of the

seventeenth Parliament of the United Kingdom, 41 Geo. III.
to 22 Vict. (1801–1859). Compiled by order of the Select
Committee on the Library of the House of Lords. 1860.
Folio, pp. 992.

House of Lords.—A General Index to the Sessional Papers, printed by
order of the House of Lords or presented by Special Command, from 22 Vict. (1859) to 33 & 34 Vict. (1870). 1872.
Folio, pp. xv, 368.

Indexes are published annually in continuation of this.

House of Commons.—Indexes to the Reports of the House of Commons,
1801–1834. 10th July, 1837. Folio. pp. 88. Divided into
the following sections—"Ecclesiastical," "Education,"
"Finance and Public Accounts," "Municipal Reform,"
"Debtor and Creditor."

——— A General Index to the Reports from Committees of the House
of Commons, 1715–1801, forming the series of fifteen
volumes of Reports. [London], 1803. Folio, title, 1 leaf,
pp. 380.

——— General Index to the Reports of Select Committees, printed
by order of the House of Commons, 1801–1852. [London],
1853. Folio, pp. xxxii, 412.

——— General Index to the Reports on Public Petitions, 1833–1852.
[London], 1855. Folio, pp. xxxvi, 984.

——— General Index to the Divisions of the House of Commons,
1852-53–1857. [London], 1857. Folio, pp. x, 202.

——— General Index to the Bills, Reports, Accounts, and other
Papers, printed by order of the House of Commons,
1801–1826. [London], 1829. Folio, pp. iv, 352.
In one alphabet.

——— General Index to the Bills, Reports, Accounts, and other
Papers, printed by order of the House of Commons,
1832–1838. [London], 1840. Folio, title, 1 leaf, pp.
338.

——— General Index to the Accounts and Papers, Reports of Com-
missioners, Estimates, &c. &c., printed by order of the
House of Commons, or presented by command, 1801–1852
[London], 1853. Folio, pp. l, 1080.

——— General Index to the Bills printed by order of the House
of Commons, 1801–1852 [London], 1853. Folio, pp. xlii,
468.

——— General Index to the Bills, Reports, Accounts, and other Papers
printed by order of the House of Commons or presented

by command, 1852–53–1861. 8 April, 1862. Folio, Pp. lxii, 1019.

House of Commons.—General Index to the Bills, Reports, Estimates, Accounts and Papers printed by order of the House of Commons, and to the Papers presented by command, 1852–53–1868–69 [London], 1870. Folio, title, pp. 775.

Charities.—Index to the Reports of the Commissioners for inquiring Concerning Charities in England and Wales. London, 1840. Folio, title, pp. 443.

Historical MSS.—Fourth Report of the Royal Commission on Historical Manuscripts. Part ii, Index, 1874. Folio, pp. 615–985.

———— Fifth Report. Part ii, Index, 1876. Folio, pp. 659–985.

———— Sixth Report. Part ii, Index, 1878. Folio, pp. 783–958.

    References are made in this index to the columns as well as to the pages, the columns being designated by the letters *a, b.*

London Corporation.—An analytical index of the minutes of Evidence taken before the Commissioners appointed to Enquire into the state of the Corporation of the City of London, etc., etc., etc., 1854. Pp. 879–1058.

Standards.—General Index to the Reports of the Standards Commission (Reports I. to V.). London, 1878. Folio, pp. viii, 101. In one alphabet, with a preliminary list of the entries.

INDEXES TO PROCEEDINGS OF PUBLIC BODIES.

Boston [*Mass.*] (*City of*).—Index to the City Documents, from 1834 to 1865. Boston, 1866. pp. 39.

———— from 1834 to 1874. Boston, 1875.

Canada.—General Index to the Journals of the Legislative Assembly of Canada, in the 1st, 2nd, and 3rd Parliaments, 1841–1851. By Alfred Todd. Montreal, 1855. fol. pp. 575.

Courts of Equity, etc.—An Index to all the reported Cases decided in the several Courts of Equity in England and Ireland, the Privy Council, and the House of Lords; and to the Statutes on or relating to the Principles, Pleading and Practice of Equity and Bankruptcy; from the earliest period. By Edward Chitty. In four volumes. London, 1853. 8vo. In double columns.

Rotuli Parliamentorum.—Index to the Rolls of Parliament, comprising the Petitions, Pleas and Proceedings of Parliament, from Ann. 6 Edw. I. to Ann. 19 Hen. VI. (A.D. 1278– A. D. 1503). Prepared and edited by order of a Committee of the House of Lords, in part by the Rev. John Strachey and the Rev. John Pridden, and completed by Edward Upham. London, 1832. folio, title, preface 1 leaf, pp. 1036.

> In one alphabet.

Scotland, Free Church.—Handbook and Index to the principal acts of assembly of the Free Church of Scotland, 1843–1868. Edinburgh, 1869. 12mo. pp. 63.

——— *Parliaments.*—General Index to the Acts of the Parliaments of Scotland, to which is prefixed a supplement to the Acts printed by authority of the Lords Commissioners of Her Majesty's Treasury. H. M. General Register House, Edinburgh, M.DCCC.LXXV. large folio, preface, etc., x. Chronological Table of the supplement to the Acts of the Parliament of Scotland, xi. pp. xxiii, 1255.

> In double columns.

MISCELLANEOUS INDEXES.

Augmentation Office.—Index to Particulars for Grants in the Augmentation Office, temp. Edward VI. folio, n.d. or place, pp. 28.

> Privately printed by Sir Thomas Phillipps.

Cartularies.—Index to Cartularies, since the Dissolution of Monasteries. Typis Medio-Montanis, impressit G. Gilmour, 1839. 12mo.

> Privately printed by Sir Thomas Phillipps.

County Visitations.—Indexes to the County Visitations in the Library at Middle Hill, 1840, and to a few others in the Harl. MSS., British Museum, the Bodleian Library and Queen's College, Oxford. Typis Medio-Montanis, impressit C. Gilmour, 1841. folio, pp. 56.

> By Sir Thomas Phillipps, privately printed.

English Language. — A Glossarial Index to the Printed English Literature of the Thirteenth Century. By Herbert Coleridge. London (Trübner & Co), 1859. 8vo. pp. viii, 103.

Heirs-at-Law.—Index to Heirs-at-Law, Next of Kin, Legatees,

Missing Friends, Encumbrances, and Creditors, or their representatives in Chancery suits, who have been advertised for during the last 150 years, containing upwards of 50,000 names relating to vast sums of unclaimed money. Collected, compiled, and alphabetically arranged by Robert Chambers. Third edition. London (Reeves & Turner), 1872. 8vo.

The advertisements are only referred to by numbers, and further information must be obtained from the compiler. It is therefore not a true Index, but only a means for the obtaining of money by the compiler.

Heirs-at-Law.—De Bernardy's Index Register for Next-of-Kin, Heirs-at-Law, Prize Captors, and of Unclaimed Property. 1754–1856.

India.—Index to Books and Papers on the Physical Geography, Antiquities, and Statistics of India. By George Buist, LL.D. Bombay, 1852. 8vo. pp. 103.

In one alphabet. Chiefly consisting of references to Indian periodicals.

Irish Law.—A Digest and Index of all the Irish Reported Cases in Law and Equity, from the earliest period to the present time, and also of the Reported Cases in Ecclesiastical and Criminal Law. . . . . By John Finlay, LL.D. Dublin (J. Cumming), 1830. 8vo. pp. xix, 600.

Leases.—Index of Leases of Manors and Lands in England granted since the Reformation, Annis 4 & 5 Edw. VI. [Edited by by Sir Thomas Phillipps.] 1832.

Manuscripts.—Guide to the Historian, the Biographer, the Antiquary, the man of literary curiosity, and the collector of autographs towards the verification of Manuscripts, by reference to engraved facsimiles of handwriting. [By Dawson Turner.] Yarmouth (C. Sloman), 1848. Roy. 8vo. pp. xii, 96.

A most valuable alphabetical Index of the names of celebrated men, with references to the books where specimens of their writing can be found.

Pedigrees.—Index to the Heralds' Visitations in the British Museum. 1823. 12mo. pp. 52.

—— An Index to the Pedigrees and Arms contained in the Heralds' Visitations and other Genealogical Manuscripts in the British Museum, by R. Sims. London (J. Russell Smith), 1849. Pp. vi, 330.

The names are arranged in alphabet under each county.

Pedigrees.—An Index to the Pedigrees contained in the Printed Heralds'- Visitations, etc., etc. By George W. Marshall, LL.M., of the Middle Temple. London (R. Hardwicke), 1866. 8vo. pp. 164.

An Index of the Pedigrees in Berry's County Genealogies is incorporated with this Index.

—————— Coleman's General Index to Printed Pedigrees, which are to be found in all the principal County and Local Histories and in many privately printed Genealogies, under alphabetical arrangement, with an Appendix commencing at page 106. London (J. Coleman), 1866. Pp. vii, 155.

This Index is said in the preface to contain references to nearly 10,000 pedigrees.

—————— An Index to Printed Pedigrees contained in County and Local Histories, the Heralds' Visitations, and in the more important Genealogical Collections. By Charles Bridger. London (J. Russell Smith), 1867. 8vo. pp. vi, 384.

Contains separate Indexes to family names in 287 books, and a general Index referring back to these.

Periodicals.—An Alphabetical Index to Subjects treated in the Reviews and other Periodicals, to which no indexes have been published. Prepared for the Library of the Brothers in Unity, Yale College. [By Wm. Fred. Poole.] New York, 1848. Pp. 155. In one alphabet.

—————— An Index to Periodical Literature. By Wm. Fred. Poole. New York, 1853. Roy. 8vo. pp. xi, 521.

In one alphabet of subjects.

—————— Catalogue of Scientific Papers (1800–1863). Compiled and published by the Royal Society of London. London, 1867–72. 6 vols., 4to. (1864–1873.) Vol. 7, 1877.

Vol. 1, A–Clu, pp. lxxix, 960 ; Vol. 2, Coa–Gra, pp. iv, 1012; Vol. 3, Gre–Lez, pp. v, 1002; Vol. 4, Lhe–Poz, pp. iv, 1006; Vol. 5, Pra–Tiz, pp. iv, 1000; Vol. 6, Tka–Zyl, pp. xi, 763 ; Vol. 7, A–Hyr, pp. xxxi, 1047.

The celebrated Dr. Thomas Young published in the second volume of his *Course of Lectures on Natural Philosophy and the Mechanical Arts* (1807) a most valuable Catalogue of books and papers relating to the subject of his Lectures, which is classified minutely, and occupies 514 quarto pages in double columns. In Kelland's new edition (1845) the references are abridged and inserted after the several lectures to which they refer.

Places.—Index Villaris, or an Exact Register, alphabetically digested, of all the cities, market-towns, parishes, villages . . . [in England and Wales. By J. Adams.] London, 1690. Folio, title, 3 preliminary leaves, pp. 419.

In one alphabet, with appendix.

——— Index to the Population Tables of England and Wales and Islands in the British Seas [of the Census of 1871]. Folio, pp. 570–772.

——— Alphabetical Index to the Townlands and Towns of Ireland, showing the number of the sheet of the Ordnance Survey Maps on which they appear; also the area of the Townlands, the County, the Barony, Parish, Poor Law Union, and Poor Law Electoral Division in which they are situated; and the volume and page of the Census of 1871, part 1, which contain the population and number of houses in 1841, 1851, 1861, and 1871. and the Poor Law Valuation in 1871; with separate Indices of the Parishes, Baronies, Poor Law Unions (or Superintendent Registrars' Districts), Poor Law Electoral Divisions, Dispensary (or Registrars') Districts, Petty Sessions Districts, and Parliamentary Boroughs of Ireland. Presented to both Houses of Parliament by command of Her Majesty. Dublin, 1877. Folio, pp. 799.

Records.—An Index to the Records, with Directions to the several Places where they are to be found, and short explanations of the different kinds of Rolls, Writs, etc.; to which is added A List of the Latin Sir-Names, and Names of Places, as they are written in the old Records, explained by the Modern Names. Also A Chronological Table, shewing at one View the Year of our Lord, answering to the particular year of each King's Reign, the several Parliaments, and the different Titles by which our Kings are styled in the Records. London (G. Hawkins), 1739. 8vo. pp. viii, 182.

——— Index to Records called the Originalia and Memoranda on the Lord Treasurer's Remembrancer's Side of the Exchequer, extracted from the Records, and from the MSS. of Mr. Tayleure, Mr. Madox and Mr. Chapman. . . . By Edward Jones, Inner Temple. London, Printed for the Editor, 1793, vol. 1. 1795, vol. 2. Folio.

——— An Index drawn up about 1629 of many Records of Charters granted by the different sovereigns of Scotland between

the years 1309 and 1413, most of which Records have
been long missing. With an Introduction. . . . by
William Robertson. Edinburgh (Murray & Cochrane),
1798. 4to. pp liii, 196.

Records.—Index to the Printed Reports of Sir Francis Palgrave, K.H.,
the Deputy-Keeper of the Public Records, 1840–1861.
London (Eyre & Spottiswoode), 1865, pp. 371. By John
Edwards and Edward James Tabrum. In one alphabet.

Religious Houses.—Fasti Monastici Aevi Saxonici : or an Alphabetical
List of the Heads of Religious Houses in England previous
to the Norman Conquest ; to which is prefixed a Chronological Catalogue of Contemporary Foundations. By
Walter De Gray Birch. London (Taylor & Co.), 1873. 8vo.

Sermons.—An Index to the Sermons published since the Restoration,
pointing out the texts in the order they lie in the Bible ;
showing the occasion on which they were preached, and
directing to the volume and page where they occur.
London (J. Newbery, etc.), 1751. 8vo. pp. iv, 212.
Arranged according to the order of the Books of the Bible.

——— The Preacher's Assistant. In two parts. Part 1, A Series of
the Texts of all the Sermons and Discourses preached
upon, and published since, the Restoration to the present
time. Part 2, An Historical Register of all the Authors
in the Series, containing a succinct view of their several
works. To which are added two Lists of the Archbishops
and Bishops of England and Ireland from 1660 to 1753,
with an appendix to each part. By Sampson Letsome,
M.A., Vicar of Thame, in Oxfordshire. London, 1753.
8vo. pp. xii, 288 ; part 2, title, pp. 238.

——— The Preacher's Assistant (after the manner of Mr. Letsome).
. . . . . By John Cooke, M.A. . . Rector of Wentnor,
Salop. Vol. 1. Oxford (Clarendon Press), 1783. Pp. xii,
487.
An Historical Register of all the Authors in the Series,
alphabetically disposed. Vol. 2, pp. 425.

——— The Churchman's Guide : a copious Index to Sermons and
other Works. By John Forster, M.A. London, 1840. 8vo.
List of Authors of Miscellaneous Sermons, pp. 6 Index
of Subjects, pp. 210.

——— Cyclopædia Bibliographica. . . . By James Darling. Subjects :
Holy Scriptures. London (Darling), 1859. Roy. 8vo.
Contains an Index of Sermons arranged under the texts.

Theology.—Theological Index. References to the Principal Works in every department of Religious Literature, embracing nearly 70,000 citations, alphabetically arranged under 2000 heads. By Howard Malcom, D.D., LL.D. Boston (Gould & Lincoln). 8vo. pp. 488.

> A second edition has been published.

—— Index to Systematic Theology. By Charles Hodge, D.D. London and Edinburgh, 1873. 8vo.

> pp. 79 in double cols.

Wills.—An Index to Wills proved in the Court of the Chancellor of the University of Oxford, and to such of the records and other instruments and papers of that Court as relate to matters or causes testamentary. By the Rev. John Griffiths, M.A., Keeper of the Archives. Oxford (University Press), 1862. Roy. 8vo. pp. xiv, 88.

> In one alphabet, with a chronological list appended.

INDEXES TO CATALOGUES.

British Catalogue.—Index to the British Catalogue of Books published during the years 1837 to 1857 inclusive. By Sampson Low. 1858. 8vo.

> pp. 292, xxx, and xlviii, in double columns, really compiled by Dr. Crestadoro, Librarian of the Manchester Free Library.

—— An Index to Current Literature, comprising a Reference to Author and Subject of Every Book in the English Language, and to Articles in Literature, Science and Art in Serial Publications, 1859, 1860, 1861. London (Sampson Low, Son, & Co., 47 Ludgate Hill), 1862.

> This most valuable Index was published quarterly; its failure is a loss to literature, for it was very carefully compiled.

London Catalogue of Books.—Classified Index, 1814 to 1846. London (Hodgson), 1848. 8vo.

—— 1816 to 1851. London (Hodgson), 1853. 8vo.

College of Surgeons.—Classified Index to the Catalogue of the Library of the Royal College of Surgeons. London, 1853. 8vo.

Lambeth Library.—An Index of such English Books printed before the year 1600 as are now in the Archiepiscopal Library at Lambeth. Published by . . the Rev. S. R. Maitland,

Librarian.　London (F. & J. Rivington), 1845.　8vo.
pp. xii, 120.

Med. and Chir. Soc.—Index to the Catalogue of the Library of the
Royal Medical and Chirurgical Society of London, containing an alphabetical List of Subjects, with the names
of the authors. [By B. R. Wheatley.]　London (J. E.
Adlard), 1860.　8vo. pp. vii, 293.

A new Catalogue and a new Index are now in the press.

New York State Library.—Subject - Index of the General Library.
Albany, 1872.　8vo. pp. xviii, 651.

Trin. Coll. Camb.—An Index to such English Books printed before
the year 1600 as are now in the Library of Trinity College,
Cambridge. By Edward Cranwell, Under Librarian. Cambridge, 1847.　8vo.　pp. 68.

MANUSCRIPTS.

Baker MSS.—Index to the Baker MSS., by Four Members of the
Cambridge Antiquarian Society.　1848.　8vo.

Bodleian Library.—Index to the Catalogue of the Manuscripts of Elias
Ashmole preserved in the Ashmolean Museum, and now
deposited in the Bodleian Library, Oxford.　By the Rev.
W. D. Macray.　Oxford, 1866.　4to. pp. 188 in triple
cols.

In one alphabet.

—— —— Index to the Catalogue (vols. 1 and 2) of the Rawlinson MSS.
in the Bodleian Library.　By the Rev. W. D. Macray.
Oxford, 1878.　4to. pp. 565–992.

British Museum.—Index to the Additional MSS. with those of the
Egerton Collection, 1783–1835.　London, 1849, fol.　pp.
iv, 514.

—— —— Indexes to the Additional MSS, 1836–1845.　London.　folio.

—— —— Preface and Index to the Catalogue of the Harleian MSS.
London, 1763.　fol.

INDEX.

STEPHEN AUSTIN AND SONS, PRINTERS, HERTFORD.

For EU product safety concerns, contact us at Calle de José Abascal, 56–1°,
28003 Madrid, Spain or eugpsr@cambridge.org.

www.ingramcontent.com/pod-product-compliance
Ingram Content Group UK Ltd.
Pitfield, Milton Keynes, MK11 3LW, UK
UKHW012338130625
459647UK00009B/375